Money

Banker's deception

SHAHID HASSAN
Gallian

Senior School
PEAKE HOUSE 1960-63

SANG-E-MEEL PUBLICATIONS
25, SHAHRAH-E-PAKISTAN (LOWER MALL) LAHORE.

332.1 Shahid Hassan
        Money Banker's deception/ Shahid
        Hassan.-Lahore: Sang-e-Meel Publications,
        2012.
            155pp.
            1. Banking system.   I. Title.

2012
Published by:
Niaz Ahmad
Sang-e-Meel Publications,
Lahore.

ISBN-10: 969-35-2508-6
ISBN-13: 978-969-35-2508-3

Sang-e-Meel Publications
25 Shahrah-e-Pakistan (Lower Mall), Lahore-54000 PAKISTAN
Phones: 92-423-722-0100 / 92-423-722-8143 Fax: 92-423-724-5101
http://www.sang-e-meel.com e-mail: smp@sang-e-meel.com
PRINTED AT: HAJI HANIF & SONS PRINTERS, LAHORE.

Dedication

This book is dedicated to the memory of my mother, HAMEEDA, who single handedly brought us up [4 sons & 1 daughter] in most trying circumstances with a will of a superwoman. Thank you, Ammi.

Contents

Preface

Seeing the general poverty and lack of infrastructure in Pakistan, I was intrigued at the indifference of the government of the day for its inability to address the problem when the country was more than self sufficient in an important factor of production, namely labour, which remained largely idle and that too in an agricultural economy. The government, in justification of its inaction, would always claim lack of 'money' as its rationale for the dismal situation.

The issue of lack of 'money' led me to research the aspect of money in all its manifestations. I spent a number of years in acquiring books, some 'out of print', and their study to fathom the mystery of money. To my surprise, it transpired that the issue of money was in fact very simple and straightforward; yet it was deliberately made to look complex and beyond the comprehension of the generally educated populace by the so-called specialists with a view to perpetuate the mystery surrounding the subject, which is so even today in the 21st century.

The governments, constituted the world over always as dictatorships of either the voting majority of the electorate for a certain period of time or of powerful elites endlessly or longer periods of time, be it military or otherwise, has within its powers, as sovereign authority, to levy taxes, in kind or cash, latter currently, on the population to meet its expenditures; yet appears incapable, in replacement of the barter mechanism of exchange, to issue a neutral medium of exchange- money, which in its totality for the whole economy, has to be borrowed into existence from the banking system, be it the central bank and/or the commercial banks.

About this 'borrowing or credit', the American economist Garet Garrett once wrote; *"of all the discoveries and inventions by which we live and die, this totally improbable helix of credit is the most cunning, the most liable, the least comprehended and next to high explosives, the most dangerous."* How dangerous this borrowing / credit has become for the governments is evidenced in the current SOVEREIGN DEBIT CRISIS of the Euro zone , USA & UK-the most economically advanced countries of the world.

The global debt crisis of 2008 was largely restricted to the private debt which had ballooned to unsustainable levels leading to near collapse of the western financial system. This crisis was averted by the intervention of the concerned governments who had injected large dozes of cash into the banking system to supplement their depleted capital reserves. What is ironic in this exercise is that the 'cash' that the governments had injected was also borrowed into existence from the banking system; the exercise leading to a partial transfer of outstanding private debt to public debt. Three years down the road, we are now confronted with sovereign - debt crisis which again threatens the viability of the western banking system.

What then is the debt crisis of the banking system? Since money creation is the prerogative of the banking system - (central and commercial banks)- and is created by the process of loans giving rise to debt; it is inevitable that the growth of an economy, measured with reference to Gross Domestic Product, GDP will move in direct proportion to the growth of debt, for obviously lack of money- a neutral medium of exchange, will impede growth.

It is axiomatic, under the circumstances, to question growth of debt in an expanding economy; yet the financial crisis of 2008 & 2011 have, at its very base, the question of sustainability of debt, be that of private or public. All economic measurements, in this regard, are limited to ratio assessment of 'debt to GDP', which on close examination is self contradictory- especially in the case of sovereign debt.

In conventional economics, it is said that 'inflation' is the consequence of too much money chasing too few goods and vice versa 'deflation' where many goods are chasing less money. In this context, the principal role for monetary policy is the maintenance of price stability which it tries to attend to with reference to the aggregate quantity of money in the economy. If there is to be no inflation/ no deflation with a view to maintaining price stability, it is incumbent that the aggregate goods in an economy must be equal to gross money circulating in the economy. Goods (and services) are measured with reference to GDP and aggregate money with reference to aggregate broad money supply M2 – in our money supply equation. Hence, we have an equality GDP=M2 for meeting the goal of price stability.

It is indeed strange that all economic analysis that are currently being churned out by our academics and media, with reference to current monetary crisis, is limited in scope to an assessment of the viability of debt to GDP and not with reference to M2 to GDP- the latter being more of essence than the former. Debt viability is limited in scope for it is primarily related to the interests of the banking system whereas assessment of M2 vis-à-vis GDP is of much more relevance, in that it has implications for the economy, as a whole and price level in particular. And, of course, if banking interests are to supersede that of national interests, then curtailment of debt, per se, will, as an off set, contract the economy, as is being evidenced in the GREEK sovereign debt crisis. The proposal to reduce budget deficits, as an austerity measure, is fueling recession in the country which in turn is causing slippages in the implementation targets negotiated with IMF, ECB and EU in support of the financial accommodation provided by these organizations, causing a rethink in the Euro zone as how best to attend to the sovereign debt crisis.

It is crisis, such as these, which need a wholesome rethink of economic paradigm for the future, if human race is to surmount the 'self destruct' mechanism embedded in the existing economic order, particularly the monetary system. To do so, one needs to have a comprehensive understanding of the issue of money, its forms and its creation and hence this research study, which I hope will go some way in enlightening the reader of the real facts as opposed to the fictional.

In the end, I would like to acknowledge with gratitude the persistent promptings of my friend and colleague, Siyyid Tahir Nawazish, to reduce my views into writing without whose encouragement, perhaps, I would not have mustered the courage for this exercise; my sister, Yasmeen Akhtar for the initial review and comments on the manuscript. Her comments and suggestions encouraged me to improve upon the text in a meaningful manner. Last but not the least, I am most gratefully indebted to my colleague of long association Syed Muhammad Azimuddin who had transferred the manuscript, written in a difficult-to-read hand writing, into a readable type script with many repeats and my colleague Farhat Ullah Siddiqui for assisting in the review of figures and preparing graphs for chapter 9.

Shahid Hassan

Karachi

September 2011

Foreword

Money - Banker's Deception by Shahid Hassan is an outstanding book. It has been written at just the right time and is highly relevant to problems confronting, not just Pakistan, but the overwhelming majority of countries in the world. It has now become abundantly clear that for the past two centuries, and even more, global politics has been increasingly controlled by a cabal of families known euphemistically as "international bankers".

These families have managed to amass astounding wealth over the course of time and understand more about financial manipulation than any other organized group. Things have come to such a pass that David Icke has been forced to state: "Money is a nonexistent theoretical force that has never, does not, and will never exist, except in theory on computer screens. People die and starve because they don't have enough digits on the screen!" Governments, lawmakers and academia works for this cabal.

It has been pointed out by Dean Henderson that these banking families, apart from owning all major banks and all major oil companies, are among the top ten shareholders in each of the Fortune 500 companies. It may be borne in mind that in 2009, among the top 100 economic entities in the world, there were 44 corporations. These families own the central banks of numerous countries such as USA, UK, etc – the equivalents of the State Bank of Pakistan – and issue currency, such as Federal Reserve notes (known as dollars) and give this currency to the government as debt! Interest is charged on this debt twenty four hours a day, seven days a week!

Once these facts are kept in view it automatically becomes clear who really runs the world. The GDP of USA is around 14-15 trillion dollars and the debt owed by the US Government to the privately owned Federal Reserve is now equal to the GDP. There is no way the people of the US can now repay this loan. As long as the present system exists the US shall remain in the bondage of the banking cabal. (What is a 'failed state'? The phrase 'failed state' is used by the US Government for other countries). The goal of these banking families is a One World Government under their control. This is the New World Order. It all boils down to an understanding of Money. Mr. Shahid Hassan's book deals with this vital subject.

The unrest among the American youth is the result of the debt burden carried by the Americans individually and collectively. This burden has been imposed as a matter of well thought out policy on the part of the "international bankers" as a part of their design to enslave the globe by enslaving the US public. US media, which is owned by a handful of major corporations, has ridiculed the Occupy Wall Street (OWS) Movement. Decreased higher education affordability is an integral part of this long term strategy. It has been pointed out by Stephen Lendman that at least "two thirds of the class of 2010 graduated with student debt, besides others incurred for them by parents or other family members." The tuition fees in UK universities have been increased by law makers despite widespread protests. The banking cabal wants the younger generation to live under eternal debt bondage so that it can be controlled.

Mr. Shahid Hassan is eminently qualified to write such a book. He is a graduate in Economics and Internationals Relations, an ideal combination for understanding the interaction of finance and global politics, and has a banking career spanning 42 years. He has worked in several major banks, including banks owned by the "international bankers". He has therefore watched the financial operations of banks with a global reach and deep history, from close quarters. As he puts it (emphasis in original): "Since the whole world economy is debt based, where money comes into existence through debt rather than through savings, it would be self-contradictory for the IMF to effectively reduce World's outstanding aggregate debts for such a policy would adversely affect the 'Money Lords'...".

Mr. Shahid Hassan has written this concise book with great clarity and I would unhesitatingly recommend it to every reader with an interest in the woes afflicting mankind. It is the duty of everyone to acquire an understanding of the money question. I would particularly recommend it to the younger generation. It will lead us to an understanding of how the globe is controlled by the "international bankers" and point out the key group behind almost all major global upheavals, including world wars and so called revolutions. Such understanding may eventually show the younger generation the path to restoration of the human scale and the rebuilding of society on humane principles. The other options are eternal bondage under what Winston Churchill called the "High Cabal" or eventual extinction of mankind in a nuclear holocaust.

Prof. Dr. Mujahid Kamran
Vice Chancellor
University of the Punjab, Lahore
November 20, 2011

Chapter I

Forms of Money and it's Creation

"The study of money is an absolute novelty to most people and their preconceptions, derived from undue absorption in its individual acquisition, make it a difficult subject, the more so as very powerful vested interest depends for their continued existence upon the public being kept in ignorance of its mysteries".

Prof. F. Soddy – Nobel Laureate.

An attempt is being made to unravel the mysteries of the monetary system by exploring the subject in its very basics.

To begin with, in the context of Pakistan, let us see what is called money in its various forms and how it comes about in existence.

State Bank of Pakistan (SBP), Pakistan's Central bank, states with respect to bank notes & coins:

(a) *"The liability of the Bank towards bank notes issued as LEGAL TENDER under the State Bank of Pakistan Act, 1956 is stated at the face value and is represented by the specified assets of the ISSUE DEPARTMENT of the bank. The cost of printing of notes is charged to the profit & loss account as and when incurred.*

(b) The Bank also issues coins of various denominations on behalf of the Government of Pakistan (GOP). These coins are PURCHASED from the GOP at their respective face values."

The points arising from the foregoing quotations are:

(1) Issuance of notes by the bank is the LIABILITY OF THE BANK;

(2) The bank notes so issued shall be the LEGAL TENDER at any place in Pakistan. They shall, however, be 'guaranteed' by the Federal Government (Section 25 of SBP Act, 1956);

(3) The bank shall have the sole right to issue bank notes. As an exception, *"Currency notes of the GOVERNMENT OF PAKISTAN supplied to the bank by the Government may be issued by it (SBP) for a period which shall be fixed by the Federal Government on the recommendation of the Central Board"* (Section 24 of SBP Act, 1956).

(4) Assets of the ISSUE DEPARTMENT OF SBP:

The assets of the Issue Department shall not be less than the total of its liabilities and shall be maintained as follows;

(i)   gold coins, gold bullion, silver bullion;

(ii) special drawings rights held with IMF;

(iii) approved foreign exchange;

(iv) rupee coins;

(v) rupee securities of any maturity;

(vi) eligible promissory notes & bills of exchange (Section 30 of SBP Act, 1956).

As for the LIABILITIES OF THE ISSUE DEPARTMENT, these shall be an amount equal to the total of the amount of the bank notes for the time being in circulation (Section 32 of SBP Act 1956) and concerning the ISSUE DEPARTMENT of the Bank, it shall be responsible for the issuance of bank notes. This department shall be separated & kept wholly distinct from the Banking Department and the assets of the Issue Department shall not be subject to any liability other than the liabilities of this department (Section 26 of the SBP Act 1956).

(5) The bank will issue coins on BEHALF OF THE GOVERNMENT which it shall purchase from GOP at face value.

Money in the form of Legal Tender (currency notes) – a liability of the issue department of SBP, is backed up by assets of the issue department of SBP comprising, principally, of the following:

(a) Gold / Silver

(b) approved foreign exchange (Reserves)

(c) IMF's SDRs

(d) Securities

The latter appear under the head 'Investment' – Asset of the issue department and comprise of Market Treasury Bills issued by GOP (giving an annual return for the year 2008 – 09 @ 11% - 14% pa).

There are no upper or lower limits prescribed for these assets by the Act.   So, the elements backing the monetary base could vary over time and theoretically, all the assets [100%] can comprise of government securities [In the case of Bank of England, its note issue, in the issue department, (liability) is represented by government securities to the extent of 100% on the asset side] or various percentage combinations amongst the various defined assets.

For instance, SBP Annual Report (2008 – 09) as at 30th June, 2009 displays the following situation with respect to the affairs of its issue department.

Liabilities	Assets	
Rs.1,223,717,612 (notes issued)	Gold	157,543,551
	Foreign Currency reserves	378,121,342
	SDR (IMF)	6,318,150
	Investments *	674,410,375
	Miscellaneous items	7,321,194
Rs.1,223,717,612		Rs.1,223,717,612

The percentage back up of various assets against the total value of notes issued–liability is:

Gold	:	12.87%
FEX Reserve	:	30.90%
Investments	:	55.11%
SDR (IMF)	:	0.52%
Miscellaneous	:	0.6 %

100 %

Position as at 30th June, 2008 was:

Liabilities	Assets		
Rs.1,046,039,412 (notes issued)			
	Gold	Rs. 130,970,552	12.50%
	FEX Reserves	Rs. 439,104,769	42.00%
	Investments*	Rs. 458,259,765	43.81%
	SDR (IMF)	Rs. 11,632,215	1.11%
	Misc items	Rs. 6,072,111	0.58%
		Rs.1,046,039,412	100 %

* Investments : Rupee Securities (Market Treasury Bills).

Ignoring SDRs & Miscellaneous items [for their relatively small amounts), the principal assets backing the notes issue are:

a) Government securities, earning for the holder / SBP a return at current market rates applicable for treasury bills;

b) Foreign exchange reserves (valued: mark to market);

c) Gold reserves (valued: mark to market);

The issue of 'government securities' merit special consideration, because this is the principal tool available to the government to expand or reduce the aggregate 'note issue' – the legal tender, at will, in the absence of any defined mandated percentage limit of the legal tender at any given time. Barring significant changes in the other components. *"the supply of money is not dependent on any other factor of the economy and is simply what the central authorities want it to be" Lipsey – Introduction to Positive Economics.* In support of the foregoing quotation, the growth of M2 (Broad Money) vis-à-vis GDP, at constant factor cost 1999 / 2000, in the case of Pakistan, has risen from 15% in 1990 to 102% in 2010, and, in terms of market price, had ranged between 39% to 50% for the same period.

Operating via the issue department of the central bank, where equality of assets to liabilities has to be maintained, the government, in seeking to raise any amount of legal tender, in effect ends up 'borrowing' from the central bank against the security of its financial paper called the Treasury Bill (government security) provided there are no meaningful positive changes in foreign exchange reserves and or gold reserves to offset the need for additional legal tender.

These Treasury Bills earn for the central bank market based returns. In consequence standard debtor / creditor banking relationship comes into effect where government is the debtor and the central bank is the creditor giving rise to what is called a 'National Debt' whose servicing (interest/ return payments) the government finances through taxation..

Through the aforesaid procedure, money, in the form of legal tender, comes into existence as DEBT where every note in circulation has an element of 'interest' associated with it.

Can a 'debt based' system for the issuance of legal tender be avoided given recourse to other options namely foreign exchange reserves and / or gold reserves?

Let us examine the aspect of gold reserves. These can be accumulated provided the country has recourse to its unlimited supply. This is not possible as the gold reserves, in mines world – wide, have only a determinate quantity provided by nature and will operate as a brake in the continuing expansion of money supply for a growing economy. It has, as a result, ceased to be an adequate back up for the paper based legal tender and therefore the abolition of the so-called 'Gold standard' from the economy of the world.

In so far as foreign exchange reserves are concerned, these can be accumulated by a country in its international trading activities by having net surplus in its balance of payment, which should continue indefinitely, which is not possible for it entails that some other countries / trading partners must be in perpetual deficits leading to permanent imbalances in international trade / currencies across the globe.

To acquire foreign exchange reserves [for deficit countries] through borrowings in international currencies would give rise to the issue of 'national debt', this time 'international debt', with attendant interest costs and an exposure to the exchange risk for the borrower in an environment of floating exchange rate regimes.

Consequently, the only mechanism for the issuance of legal tender without recourse to 'debt' is for the country to exercise its SOVEREIGN RIGHT to issue legal tender (currency) just as the state exercises its sovereign right to levy taxes on the public.

In the context of Pakistan and with reference to the State Bank of Pakistan Act 1956 a provision, by way of an exception, is provided which reads "------ PROVIDED THAT THE CURRENCY NOTE OF THE GOVERNMENT OF PAKISTAN SUPPLIED TO THE BANK (SBP) BY THE GOVERNMENT MAY BE ISSUED BY IT FOR A PERIOD WHICH SHALL BE FIXED BY THE FEDERAL GOVERNMENT ON THE RECOMMENDATION OF THE CENTRAL BOARD (Section 24 of SBP Act 1956)."

This is indeed a very 'loaded' provision which may have escaped the attention of 'money men' too engrossed in following the usual banking practices world wide, particularly with regard to the issuance of legal tender, as debt. Let us examine the 'provision' in detail.

(a) This time the currency notes will be those of the Government of Pakistan (GOP) and not that of State Bank of Pakistan.

Since, by implication, these will be issued by GOP, the regulations applicable for issuance of legal tender via SBP's ISSUE DEPARTMENT will not apply;

(b) These notes will be SUPPLIED TO THE BANK BY THE GOVERNMENT. The 'Supply' will obviously entail handover of something physical / material i.e. printed notes and printed by the Government and handed over to SBP just as Treasury Bills are printed and provided by GOP to SBP as back up for the legal tender;

(c) Since this activity will be outside the purview of issue department there will be no need for an asset backup and the consequential interest income accruing to SBP from GOP;

(d) There will be no need for a government guarantee for the legal tender as a back up, for the legal tender now is issued by the GOVERNMENT ITSELF;

(e) The word "MAY BE ISSUED BY IT" in this context and with reference to SBP would actually mean CIRCULATED BY IT (SBP), for obviously notes issued by GOP will not, logically, be reissued by SBP, and that too bearing the imprint of GOVERNMENT OF PAKISTAN.

By availing the use of this provision, the desired quantity of legal tender will come into existence without creating a corresponding debt and the attendant servicing costs for the government.

The next question in our enquiry is to find out the extent of involvement of legal tender (currency notes) in the total money supply.

Money supply, in the monetary statistics published by State Bank of Pakistan, has been defined as:

M_2 (Board Money) = Currency in circulation + other deposits with SBP + scheduled bank's demand deposits+ scheduled bank's time deposits + Resident foreign currency deposits.

The above equation can be simplified into two principal components / variables, if one ignores the 'prefixes' attached to different forms of deposits – viz:'Other', 'Scheduled bank's demand', 'Scheduled bank's time' and 'Resident foreign currency'
Money supply equation will now read :

M_2 = Currency in circulation (C) + Deposits with the banking System (D)
or $M_2 = C + D$

Examining the figures of M2 vis-à-vis currency issued and outstanding for the period 1972 – 2005 (as of 30th June), it is observed that currency issued and outstanding ranged between 34% to 25% of the broad money M2 i.e. falling progressively over the years, implying a gradual reducing role of legal tender in the broad money supply and a corresponding increasing role of 'deposits' with the banking system. [For the UK, the equivalent role of legal tender vis-à-vis broad money supply is said to be a mere 3%].

Since 'deposits' as a consequence, constitute approximately 75% of the broad money supply (second component/variable), it is of critical importance to examine the mechanism for the creation of 'deposits' in the banking system.

In its very essence, the deposits with banking system are created from public's savings, where a depositor has a certain income of which he consumes a portion for his upkeep and sets aside the balance as his savings for the 'rainy day'. These savings he deposits with his bank in cash where the bank, in accordance with the principles of 'double entry' book keeping, records the transaction thus: (for illustration, we assume the depositor has Rs.1000 left for savings which he deposits with his bank).

Customer - A		Cash in Bank's	
Deposit Account		till _____	

Debit	Credit	Debit	Credit
	1,000.00	1,000.00	

FIG. 1.

Once again, we revert back to State Bank of Pakistan's monetary statistics for the period 1972 – 2005 (as of 30th June) and observe that the aggregate 'cash in tills' with the banking system vis-à-vis currency in circulation ranges between 6% to 7%, implying that of the aggregate currency in circulation only 6% – 7% of its total is represented by public's cash transfer to the banking system, the remaining 94% - 93% of the aggregate currency in circulation remains in the custody of the public at large – out side the banking system; perhaps signifying the 'cash liquidity preference' of the general public.

Given that 'deposits' in our case study, represent 75% of the broad money supply, of which the legal tender contributes a mere 7% to 6% of the currency in circulation, in the form of 'cash' with the banking system, as backup for deposit, the question arises as to the source 'funding' the remaining major portion (about 70%) of deposits with the banking system.

The business of banking, as we know, is to take public deposits and lend to prospective borrowers, at an interest 'spread' – the difference between the deposit rate and the lending rate – sharing the spread between the depositor and the bank, as appropriate.

Continuing with our illustration and for the sake of convenience, we will assume transactions with one bank only with the initial cash deposit of Rs.1000 by a customer-A with a proviso that a bank lending customer's deposit will set aside 10% of the deposit as 'reserve', lending the balance 90% onwards. Further, a bank in the process of lending will do so only to its customer for which a Banker / Customer relationship will be entered, necessitating in the first instance, the customer opening an account with the bank, which will issue him a 'cheque book' which will facilitate withdrawals of funds from the account. The customer borrowing money from the bank is named B.

Customer-B, having opened an account with the bank, now makes a request for a loan subject to satisfying the bank with regard to security and other procedural issues.

Based on the initial deposit of customer A of Rs.1000 and assuming a reserve of 10% that the bank will keep aside, the maximum the bank can lend is Rs.900 and this is the amount B has requested. Having processed customer B's request, the bank, in disbursing the loan will record transaction # 2 as given in Fig 2, that is, the bank will create a loan account in the name of the customer B and will debit the same Rs.900/- an asset of the bank, correspondingly crediting customers B's deposit account with Rs.900 – a liability of the bank, completing the double entry transaction. This is merely a book transaction and *a deposit is created, funded by a loan in the name of customer B WITHOUT any corresponding cash inflow into the bank's till.* So, we now have two customers, A&B, whose aggregate deposits with the bank equal Rs.1900 (1000+900) against cash balance available with bank in an aggregate value of Rs.1000 [cash in till – net debit balance of Rs.900 & cash in reserve account – net debit balance of Rs.100 – Aggregate cash balance of Rs.1000]. If both the depositors, A&B, were simultaneously to withdraw their 'credit' balances from their accounts, the bank will not be able to meet the demand and will be deemed 'bankrupt' at that moment of time. However, experience, in general, shows that all the depositors do not withdraw the amounts standing to their 'credits' with their bank simultaneously unless there is a 'run' on the bank.

Theoretically, the bank, without getting any further CASH deposit, can continue with the process (note transactions # 3, 4 & 5 as given in Fig 2) lending upto Rs.9000 in aggregate against the initial cash deposit of Rs.1000 by repeating the transaction about 75 number of times, keeping aside 10% of the new deposit so created as reserve till the 'cash in till' is exhausted and is replaced by cash, in equivalent value, in the 'reserve' account of Rs.1000. ***Transactions # 2 & # 5 are transactions in deposit creation through loans – an act of money creation – loan based.***

For this repetitive exercise, we are assuming that we are still operating with one bank and that all deposits being created, subsequent to the initial 'cash' deposit of Rs.1000 are through loans and are recycled back as new deposit and re-lent again, minus the 10% reserve that is set aside, for each deposit recorded and outstanding.

Further for all transactions, save the initial one of Rs.1000, withdrawal and deposits are through cheque drawn by different customers, all banking with this one bank.

The aforesaid is illustrated thus:

Fig.2

Transaction #
1
Customer A depositing Rs.1000 with his bank in cash

LIABILITIES			ASSETS	ASSETS	
Deposit A / customer A				Cash in bank's till-----	
Debit	Credit			Debit	Credit
	1000	[deposit in cash]		1000	100
				90	90
					90
Transaction #					81

2

Customer B request for loan of
Rs.900
which the bank disburses into
his account

Deposit A/C Customer B	
Debit	Credit
	900

[loan
proceeds]

Loan A/C Customer B	
Debit	Cred it
900	

[lo
an

disbursed]

1090	361

Net debit
balance 729

Cash Reserve Account	
Debit	Credit
100	
90	90
90	
81	
361	90

Net debit
balance 271
[729 + 271 =
1000]
Aggregate Cash
(sum
total of net debit
balances)

Transaction #

3

Customer-B, through a cheque
drawn on the bank,
withdrawals his deposit and pays
the same to

Merchant C for purchases

Deposit A/C Customer B	
Debit	Credit
	B/F
900	900
XXX X	XXX X

withd
rawal

by cheque

drawn

[credit
balance
brought
forward]

Transaction #

4

Merchant - Customer C deposit
the cheque in

his account with the bank

Deposit A/C Customer C	
Debit	Credit
	900

[deposit by
cheque]

Transaction #
5
Customer D requests for loan of 810 which the
bank disburses in his
account

Deposit A/C Customer D		
Debit	Credit	
	810	[loan proceeds]

Loan A/C Customer D		
		Cred it
Debit		
[lo an	810	
disbursed]		

Total deposits outstanding	Total loans outstanding	Total Cash Outstanding
1000	900	729
+ 900	+ 810	+ 271
+ 810	1710	1000
2710		

Liabilit ies	Assets
27 10	1710 + 1000 = 2710

The following issues come to light under this process of creating multiple deposits against the initial 'cash' deposit.

The source of initial deposit is 'cash' – legal tender created as debt.

The source of second and subsequent deposits, upto about 75 such deposit transactions, are loans which are created as mere book entries with the resultant aggregate additional deposits of about Rs.9000 representing 9 times (multiple of 9) of the value of the initial cash deposit of Rs.1000.

Deposits so created and which are the components of the money supply – M2 add to the aggregate money supply M2.

This addition to money supply M2 is in effect 'deposit money creation' by the banking system, through a source called 'Loan' – a debt

This process of 'money creation' is in fact money creation out of thin air by the banking system called numbered or digital money via a tab on computer key board.

The mechanism of money creation, described above, is formally called FRACTIONAL RESERVE SYSTEM of banking and operates principally, in transferring so called 'deposit money', largely via the novel instrument introduced in the form of a CHEQUE – note transactions # 3 & # 4 (Fig 2).

Whilst there is legislation in place for the creation of 'legal tender' (SBP Act of 1956) – one form of money, what law is that lends support to the creation of 'deposit money' – the other form of money?

In examining this issue, we need to go back in history, when our forebears, the goldsmiths, originally accepted gold for safe keeping at a small fee. Against this gold deposit, the goldsmith issued receipts, gold receipts as such, upon presentation of which, the presenter could obtain physical gold of due quantity. The total number of gold receipts issued equaled the total quantity of gold held for safe keeping.

These gold receipts soon acquired acceptance in the market place for the exchange of goods and settlement thereof, obviating the need to withdraw the gold at each instance to support a trade transaction in the market place. Occasionally, however, a holder of the gold receipt would recall gold against the receipt from the goldsmith. Such physical movements, the goldsmith observed, were limited to about 10 percent of the physical gold in his care, whilst the remaining 90 percent or so gold stayed put in the vault gathering dust. This tempted the goldsmith to issue additional gold receipts, without additional gold stocks to support the same, which he on-lent to prospective borrowers at interest. It must be noted that goldsmith had no legal right to lend, at interest, against gold deposits considered surplus to the immediate requirements of the depositors. To use such deposits of physical gold for issuance of 'additional' gold receipts, in excess of the physical quantity of gold in his possession, without the express approval of the depositor was, in fact, a breach of contract of 'bailment' under which the arrangement of deposit of physical gold was entered into by the depositor – called Bailor and the goldsmith, the Bailee. This act of the goldsmith was in fact an act of DECEPTION for he was giving the impression that all gold receipt were fully [100 percent] backed by physical gold whereas in reality this was not so because he had issued additional receipts unsupported by due quantity of physical gold in his vault.

As time progressed, depositors were placing 'deposits' with their bankers (goldsmiths having graduated to this status), in cash, legal tender, and the bankers continued to lend such deposits to prospective borrowers (deposits multiplied as per practice explained in Fig 2) until 1848 when the legal relationship between the depositor and his bank came up for a detailed judicial review, a brief extract of which is quoted hereunder from L.C. Mather's classic – Banker & Customer Relationship.

"In FOLEY V. HILL (1848) 2 H.L.C. 28 a customer brought an action against a banker to account for his monies received, claiming that the relationship was equitable akin to that of principal & agent, and that he was entitled on that basis to know what had happened to his money and what profits has been derived from it. It was contended that the agency relationship

created a trust and made the banker accountable to the customer, his principal".

At this instance, "for the first time the relationship of debtor and creditor was recognized, thereby enabling the banker to use his deposits, as he may wish, being money borrowed from his customer and in full control of the banker subject always to the liability of the banker to repay the depositor".

To quote from the judgment, *"money paid into a banker is money known by the principal to be placed there for the purpose of being under the control of the banker; it is then the banker's money; he is known to deal with it as his own; he makes what profit he can, which profit he retains to himself---- he has contracted, having received the money, to repay to the principal when demanded a sum equivalent to that paid into his hands".*

So we now have a judicial ruling, having the force of law, by which the act of deception has been legalized notwithstanding that the banker becomes indebted to his customer and THAT THE ORDINARY RULE THAT A DEBTOR MUST SEEK OUT HIS CREDITOR is overturned in a banker's "DEBTOR CREDITOR RELATIONSHIP" where the onus for repayment of his money is placed on the CREDITOR requiring him to make a DEMAND on the DEBTOR in the first instance – the banker in this regard.

To further strengthen the banker in his deception, the accounting profession, through it's fabled 'double entry system', designates the 'Cash' that is deposited with the banker as an Asset of the banker whilst correspondingly recording depositor's claim as liability of the bank-a mere PROMISE TO PAY WHEN DEMANDED. From this practice, we observe that a banker may have, in aggregate, large customer's deposits shown in his balance sheet against which 'cash', as back up, represents an insignificant aggregate sum.

One may reasonably question how it is possible for bankers to continue in business given such a precarious, illiquid situation?

The institutional framework that provides liquidity to the banker, in such a scenario, comprise of:

(a) The central bank;

(b) The inter-bank money market;

(c) The clearing House;

The CENTRAL BANK acts as a 'lender of last resort' to the banks, all of whom are in an account relationship with it. As and when liquidity deficits needs funding and no other avenues are available for the same, banks can approach the central bank to have 'eligible securities' (mostly Treasury Bills) held by banks, discounted. The discounting cost is invariably kept high relative to other money market rates to avoid its misuse for ARBITRAGE purposes by the banks.

The INTER-BANK MONEY MARKET is the primary funding source that is frequently resorted to in case of liquidity short falls by banks and / or for arbitrage transactions between the banks. It lends and borrows on short term basis – from overnight for upto 1 year on secured (security based) or unsecured basis. Its lending rates are purely a function of supply and demand in an environment of a near perfect competition. The market is represented by all banks, as participants, and they engage with each other mostly through the telephonic medium, with written confirmation of deals to follow execution of deals concluded verbally (telephonic) in the first instance.

The mechanism of 'money transfers' by cheques between banks is processed through the CLEARING HOUSE on which all banks are represented as members. Each working day, the clearing house meets twice, once in the morning and the other in the afternoon. The morning session is held to process settlement of all cheques received in the Clearing House through their members and in the afternoon to have contra-settlements effected between banks in respect of cheques returned unpaid for various reasons by member banks.

By way of illustration, let us assume three members banks, A, B & C, come to the house with cheques, in their respective possession, drawn on other banks. An exchange of cheques takes place, as appropriate, and a net deficit or surplus balance is struck for each bank, which is then settled by cheque drawn by member bank on his account with the central bank in favour of each other, as applicable.

This latter transaction would affect the overall balances of the respective member banks with the central bank. It is the 'deficits' so arising in the respective accounts of concerned members banks with the central bank that needs funding. This is attended to with recourse either to interbank money market or the central bank as described above.

It will be observed that the 'money transfers' have merely led to reduction or increase in the aggregate deposits of the member banks with individual customers' accounts reflecting withdrawals / deposits as the case may be. There is no withdrawal of money, as such, from the banking system. Cash withdrawals, however, are not processed through the clearing house but rather are processed for payment at the counters or ATMs of the banks where these are offset against 'cash in tills' balances of the bank concerned.

Notice that the banker's deception of the 'money issue' is supported by the aforesaid mechanism where the principal role played is that of the inter bank money market. Should this market cease to operate, for whatever reason, the banking system's deception will come to light and the game will be exposed with dire consequences for the debt based economy. A living example of such a collapse was witnessed in the year 2009 in New York after the collapse of LEHMAN BROTHERS – America's leading investment bank which led to near closure of the New York inter bank money market compelling the federal government of United States to intervene after the failure of the American central bank – The Federal Reserve – to stem the rot, that of funding the liquidity short fall.

To SUMMARIZE then, money exists in the form of currency notes and coins – legal lender – and banker's 'promise' to repay sums (deposits) standing to customer's credit subject to depositors demand for the same and in satisfaction of the terms and conditions of the placement.

This money comes into existence, as debt, that is, it is borrowed into existence by the state as well as by the public and the enterprise from the banking system, save a very minute amount of gold that backs the currency issue.

The notes and coins come into existence via the mint / printing presses and the bank deposits through the fractional reserve banking system. Consequently 'money' is a banker's monopoly, for which he claims a benefit in the form of interest without expending any energy for its creation, which is simply created through the thin air. The banker also secures assets of the borrower largely in support of his lending activities, and technically, is the ostensible owner of nation's assets; for all money in the economy is debt based save the exception pointed out earlier. This compels one to question who is the real power that rules the world? It is well remarked by *MEYER AMSCHEL ROTHSCHILD:*

"GIVE ME CONTROL OF MONEY AND IT DOESN'T MATTER WHO MAKES THE LAW."

Good luck Sovereign Parliaments with legislative authority exercised as the will of the electorate, an empty boast really, in the absence of money control which resides elsewhere.

Chapter - II

Domestic Debt

"Money is the creature of law, and the creation of the original issue of money should be maintained as the exclusive monopoly of the national government. Money passes no value to the state other than that given to it by circulation ----------

Government, possessing the power to create and issue currency and credit as money and enjoying the right to withdraw both currency and credit from circulation by taxation and otherwise, need not and should not borrow capital at interest as a means of financing governmental work and public enterprise. The government should create, issue and circulate all the currency and credit needed to satisfy the spending power of the government and the buying power of consumers. The privilege of creating and issuing money is not only the supreme prerogative of government, but it is the government's greatest creative opportunity --------. Money will cease to be the master and become the servant of humanity. Democracy will rise superior to the money power".

Abraham Lincoln, former President of United States of America Pg 91, 1865 Senate document 23.

In Pakistan, scarcity of money has become our nation's paramount problem leading the state and the enterprise to borrow left, right and centre. The national budgets, almost always in deficits, are funded by borrowing in local and international currencies; enterprises borrow to keep their businesses running and the consumers are provided with 'consumer finance' to purchase their requirements of durable assets and meeting expenses on deferred payment basis at exorbitant interest costs (@ 3% per month or 36% per annum on borrowings outstanding under CREDIT CARDS).

To address the issue of escalating debt in the national economy, we need first to review the situation in actual setting of Public Finance and Domestic Public Debt for the Year 2010 (as of 30th June) – the period uptill which State Bank's 'handbook of statistics on Pakistan Economy' has published data.

We observe that total receipts aggregate Rs.2,051,945 million against total expenditure of Rs.2,577,020 million, leaving a deficit to be funded at Rs.525,075/- million i.e. 21% of gross expenditure.

Aggregate domestic public debt appears at Rs.4,649,592 million which if financed at about @ 14% per annum would amount to Rs.650,942 million- about 25% of gross expenditure (Debt servicing actual figures for the year 2010 have not been provided in SBP's handbook).

Domestically, the government finances its aggregate debt as PERMANENT, FLOATING & UNFUNDED debt. Whilst the components and sub-components of the aforesaid debt classification may be increasing or decreasing from year to year, the aggregate domestic debt, nevertheless, keeps on increasing, in absolute figures, year by year, which is being financed 'as a borrowing' raising the spectre of additional debt to meet its servicing cost.

Would it not be more appropriate for this domestic debt of the government to be financed from state's exercise of its sovereign right to issue / print the currency needed for the purpose, thus saving the debt servicing cost to the economy?

Let us see how this can be achieved in a step by step approach.

To begin with, currency in circulation – notes issued by the central bank as 'legal tender' needs to be replaced by Treasury Notes issued by Government of Pakistan – GOP, without back up of interest bearing market treasury bills, a component of government's 'floating debt'. The effect of this will be 'neutral' in so far as money supply is concerned but, on the contrary, will save interest expense for the government.

The other component of the floating debt namely Treasury Bills & Adhoc Treasury Bills that are regularly auctioned by SBP to banks – in essence an exercise in roll over of maturing Treasury Bills with additions as required – to enable the latter to meet their Statutory Reserve Requirements, SLR, with respect to such securities, be gradually reduced / redeemed with compensating increases in Treasury Notes of the GOP. The SLR ultimately be abolished, allowing banks the financial space to engage in their commercial activities at market risk and terms without any compulsion as to compulsory investments in government securities. To ensure that increases in the 'currency outstanding' component of money supply so arising is correspondingly compensated by equal reduction in aggregate deposits with the banking system – the other component of money supply-action be initiated by increasing cash liquidity requirement, CLR, against current deposits of banking system in due proportion, going upto 100% ultimately so as to limit the multiplication effect embodied in fractional reserve banking system.

The banks should have no complaints for loss of income in this regard as none is payable to such depositors to begin with. Current deposits will be matched with equal cash thus avoiding liquidity crisis leading to runs on the bank. To manage such accounts, the banks may recover appropriate service charges. This exercise, in totality, would effectively get rid of the 'floating debt' and of servicing (interest) cost for the GOP and will be neutral in effect on the money supply.

Permanent debt of the GOP comprising of numerous types of medium to long term government bonds & loans be progressively redeemed in cash by corresponding increases in the Treasury Notes issue of GOP with suitable amendments approved for the banking system enforcing banks to ensure that deposits placed with them for different tenors (except current accounts) must be invested by banks under an Investor / Investee relationship, implying that such investments will not create a parallel purchasing power in the hands of the depositor / investor as is currently being done under fractional reserve banking system where money is created artificially by the lending process, as explained earlier. This should cause no problem for the banking system which accepts all tenor deposits on 'profit & loss sharing' basis, save current accounts which are deemed and were once named AMANT accounts implying a banker / customer relationship of 'bailment'.

Having disposed off government debt – namely Floating Debt and Permanent Debt – by replacing these instead with a stock of Treasury Notes of GOP, we are left now with the third major component of government debt, that of 'Unfunded Debt' which comprises of deposits placed by savers in various schemes of a government institution 'National Savings'. These represent public savings which are deployed with the government for meeting its funding requirement and need to continue to encourage saving habit amongst the general public. It is to be noted, however, that public savings invested with 'National Savings' are genuine savings where the savers abstain from consumption for the duration the sums are invested and are non – inflationary given that 'National Savings' do not create artificial deposits from these initial savings through the process of 'lending' as resorted to by the banking system through the mechanism of fractional reserve banking system. 'National Savings' are not empowered to engage in 'lending' activities but can only mobilize public savings for investment, of different tenors.

A gradual implementation of the processes explained above will bring about a meaningful change in the money supply equation where the component of 'currency outstanding' – currently at about 25% of gross money supply and 'deposits with banking system' – currently at about 75% of the gross money supply will change with 'currency outstanding' increasing its percentage share vis-à-vis 'deposit with banking system' which will be reduced substantially, ultimately leading to a point of 100 PERCENT MONEY being in the form currency outstanding in the money supply equation, which would then read :

Money Supply = Currency outstanding

Because, ultimately all deposits will be cash based. In this, the government would reclaim its sovereign right to issue legal tender without associated interest expense for itself and would in effect *'not borrow capital at interest as a means of financing government works & public enterprise'* as Lincoln recommended in his *monetary policy prescription of 1865.*

To SUMMARIZE then, government finances and its funding needs to be reorganised so as to reduce and ultimately eliminate national debt and its servicing costs, latter a substantial burden on national economy.

Taking SBP's data as of June 30 2010, total domestic debt outstanding of GOP was Rs.4,649,592 million viz-a-viz M2 at Rs.5,777,231 million. Accordingly GOP's total domestic debt outstanding was 81% of M2 and the total cash in bank's till at Rs.87, 673 million represented merely 1.5% of M2. This GOP's domestic debt outstanding has its funding source in the aggregate deposits of the banking system which is the second component of Money Supply; currency outstanding being the other. When the currency issued by SBP is replaced by

Treasury Notes issued by GOP and is further added to so as to provide the cash liquidity to redeem GOP's domestic debt to a large extent [save Prize bonds & the deposits with National Savings] coupled with increase in CLR and a reduction / elimation of SLR, we will notice a fall in aggregate deposits with the banking system as a component of money supply compensating the increase in Treasury Notes of the GOP, thus leaving gross money supply unchanged, with of course some fine tuning by the central bank.

Through this exercise, we will be able to substantially reduce the national debt and its debt serving cost which, as earlier stated, represented 25% of the aggregate expenditure of the government. The current national debt will, in the change over, come to be, largely, represented by Treasury notes of GOP, without any interest / service cost for the state, which will be meeting its expenses not by borrowed funds domestically but by creating its own legal tender as a prerogative of the government to issue currency.

The proposed changes will be reflected as follows:

Instrument of National debt	Current Practice	Proposed Change	Effects /Consequences
• Currency notes (legal tender)	Issued by SBP backed by interest bearing obligations of GOP & its guarantee (represents government's floating debt)	Replaced by Treasury Notes issued by GOP with (i) no back up arrangements and (ii) no guarantee of GOP.	(i) Total elimination of service cost for GOP on the currency issued (ii) Neutral implications for money supply
• Treasury Bills & Adhoc Treasury Bills (short term)	GOP interest bearing financial paper auctioned to banks by SBP to enable banks to meet their Statutory Liquidity Reserves – SLR (represents government's floating debt)	(i) Replaced by Treasury notes issued by GOP against which maturing liabilities of TBs will be redeemed (ii) correspondingly (a) increase Cash Liquidity Reserves – CLR – against current deposits (b) reduce SLR, both in due proportion (arithmetic exercise in this regard to be fine tuned by SBP).	SBP notes / currency replaced by GOP notes thus reducing / eliminating interest expenses thereof for GOP. Neutral effect on money supply. Money Supply = Currency outstanding + deposits with banking system effect : Money supply (no change) = currency (GOP notes) Deposits with banking system.
• GOP loans / bonds / prize bonds & other GOP financial debt obligations (medium to long term)	Sold to various entities in public / private sectors to raise funds for GOP (budget deficit financing) as government's debt, interest bearing (represents government's permanent debt)	Replaced by Treasury notes issued by GOP which will go towards redeeming these outstanding GOP interest bearing obligations. Prize bonds scheme may continue for the interim.	elimination of GOP's permanent debt (ii) Neutral effect on money supply. MS = C + D (Constant)
• Deposits	Public deposits	No change	No change.

with National Savings	solicited for short / medium/long term at competitive interest rates. Banks are not eligible to invest in this avenue. (represents government's unfunded debt)	proposed. Schemes to continue for the time being.	

Chapter III

External Debt

"They no longer use bullets and ropes. They use the World Bank & IMF instead" – 　Jesse Jackson.

Borrowings in international currencies has its own unique complexities, in that, it has to be repaid in the international currencies borrowed, the creation and supply of which is in the control of the foreign nations concerned.

Whilst a via media has been recommended in the earlier chapter as to how the national debt, denominated in domestic currency, can be 'switched' with a view to reducing the incidence of the debt servicing cost, no such remedy is available for the external debts. Besides, in an environment of floating exchange rate regimes, the borrowing country is exposed to additional costs; over and above the contracted rate of interest for the loan, in the form of exchange risk particularly if the domestic currency is devaluation prone. The exchange loss, so resulting, gets reflected directly as a budgetary expense, in addition to interest cost.

Comparatively, therefore, borrowings in international 'hard' currencies may, prima-facie, appear cheaper, in interest rate terms, vis-à-vis domestic borrowings, one has nevertheless to bear in mind the projected negative adjustment on account of the fall of the exchange rate of domestic currency, - devaluation prone – versus the international currency borrowed, during the pendency / tenor of the foreign currency loan.

Pakistan took its first plunge in soliciting a foreign currency loan in September 1947, nearly a month and a half since achieving independence in August 1947, when the Quaid-e-Azam made a request to the United States for a loan of US$ 2 billion, which however, was not acceded to for being too high. Over the years, the amount was scaled down to US$ 200 million by Khawaja Nazimuddin, Prime Minister, in 1952 with justifications to equip 10 divisions army – five armored and five infantry and 15 air squadrons for a 95,000 strong army inherited from British India [Pakistan Sovereignty Lost by Shahid ur Rehman].

Pakistan's story of international indebtedness and its consequences is a sad lament of a 'prospective heaven' turned into a 'living hell' for a large segment of the population, with government's external debt liabilities standing at US$ 60 billion, which is inclusive of approximately US$ 2.4 billion added on account of multicurrency exchange loss, with no promise, whatsoever, of its liquidation in future. Debt servicing of external debt for the 6 months period (July – Dec FY11) is $ 4.22 billion with reserves at $ 17.5 billion (end Feb'11). For the 8 months period, (July – Feb Fy11) trade deficit stands at $ 10.3 billion, current account deficit at $ 98 million (Dawn – 28-3-11). Instead of making an earnest effort at reducing this debt, a new terminology has been introduced by our former imported Finance cum Prime Minister – Shaukat Aziz, that of 'sustainability of debt' where we are taught that it is alright so long as we continue to service the debt, without clarifying from where are we to acquire 'foreign currencies' to meet the servicing cost in an environment where we are confronted with deficits in our trading and current accounts of the balance of payments, which are made up by long term borrowings on capital account to 'balance' the balance of payment account, where borrowings currently aggregates to $ 60 billion. Notwithstanding, the country continues to import 'essentials' and 'non – essentials' without any qualms, whatsoever, because we have such fantastic 'reserves', at $ 17 billion, all funded through borrowings in international currencies.

In analyzing the profile of Pakistan's external debt, we observe that the major long term lenders are:

(i)   Paris Club – Bilateral – Nation to Nation and under consortium arrangements

(ii)   Multilaterals – IBRD, ADB etc

(iii) IMF

Of the aforesaid three, the most troublesome and intrusive lenders are the IBRD (World Bank) and the IMF, who, as a rule, do not offer any relief by way of write offs. Relatively, the Paris club is more accommodating in granting reliefs, in situations of economic distress, to the borrower.

IBRD, through its arm the World Bank and its sister associate, the ADB – the Asian Development Bank, have traditionally lent money, in the form of credit lines and not in cash, for national developmental activities – industrial and infra-structure. Since Musharraf's era, these development project loans have severely been curtailed and instead substituted for various 'reforms' based financial facilities. In consequence of the latter, almost all of Pakistan's public sector Development Finance Institutions (DFIs) have had their shutters pulled down thereby freezing up long term foreign currency finance for new projects with adverse effects for the growth of the local manufacturing industries.

Government of Pakistan is the direct borrower of such facilities, assuming the credit and exchange risks in full. The World Bank and

ADB are co-assessors of the 'project risk', 'procurement evaluations' and 'project monitoring' but assume no risk whatsoever. In this role, the lenders are relying on the traditional 'debtor / creditor relationship' [see chapter I for details], where creditor having lent the money is only entitled to repayment of the same plus accrued interest at agreed rate. The money so borrowed is an asset of the borrower (debtor) who is free as to its utilization. Since monies disbursed under these facilities are not in cash, but instead are 'credit line' based, where funds are directly disbursed by the lender (WB / ADB) to the supplier for the goods supplied to the local project company, the transaction is recorded as a book entry in the books of the borrower; the lender thereby ensuring proper utilization of the loan funds. Notwithstanding this latter advantage for the lender, there is no substantial change in the basic 'debtor / credit' relationship between WB / ADB and the GOP. Yet the WB / ADB have so expanded their basic role of lenders that they have become the managers of the Pakistan economy dictating policies which are harmful to Pakistan's basic economic interests, as history proves.

In cohorts with IMF, who lends in cash, exclusively for balance of payment support, their intrusive interference in Pakistan's economy has covered the sphere of:

(a) Exchange rate policy

(b) Interest rate policy & money supply

(c) Budget policy

Managing the fiscal and the monetary policies of a borrowing country with no responsibility, these agencies have become the new colonizers, ruling by remote control, ensuring that the borrower never manages to get out of the 'debt trap' that has, so meticulously, been laid out for them.

Professor **Carroll Quigley** in his book **'Tragedy & Hope'** writes about these organizations:

"Their goal is nothing less than to create a world system of financial control in private hands to dominate the political system of each country and the economy as a whole. This system (is) to be controlled in feudal fashion by the central banks of the world acting in concert, by secret agreements arrived at in frequent private meetings & conferences".

Under dictation from WB/IMF combine, as part of their Standby Arrangements, Economic Restructuring & Poverty Elimination Programms etc. Pakistan has been forced to:

(i) <u>**Devalue its currency**</u>, in implementation of the SINKING [rather than FLOATING] exchange rate regime from 1982 onwards, where the rupee's value against US Dollar has fallen from Rs.9.90 to US$ 1 (1982) to Rs.85 to US$ 1 (2010). This was ostensibly put into effect to bring about a positive change in Pakistan's trading account leading to more exports as opposed to imports. In nearly three decades, Pakistan's Trading Account continues to be in substantial deficits, partly compensated by foreign currency inward remittances by EXPAT. Pakistanis in Current Account and foreign currency loans in Capital Account of the Balance of Payments. The offset of this policy has had its greatest adverse effects reflected in the counter-part local currency funding cost, at the time of repayment, computed at current exchange rate vis-à-vis the exchange rate applied at the time these foreign currency borrowed funds were absorbed in the domestic economy, thus increasing substantially the expenditure side of the national budget year by year.

(ii) **Implement tight Monetary Policy** by jacking up interest rates with the aim of making 'credit' dearer, thus curtailing growth in money supply and reining in inflation. Once again, this policy prescription has been found to stand upon its head when reviewed for its actual consequences. In a debt based economy, where even the legal tender comes into existence, as debt, save the minute component of its backing by gold in the overall M2 perspective, increases in interest rates shores up the cost of existing money supply, all debt based, which ultimately reflects in higher product /

service cost of goods and services in the economy which fuels further inflation rather than cause it to dampen. And the intention of the policy to curtail further 'credit' by making it expensive is of no real consequence in the absence of scientific determination of the 'elasticity' for borrowings in the economy. In any event, the amount of credit that is proposed to be so curtailed will only represent a small fraction of aggregate money supply which will definitely outweigh the adverse consequences of a general price increase in the economy, as a consequence of higher interest rate on the existing outstanding debt. Furthermore, increases in interest rate would cause shift of funds from productive enterprises to speculative purposes – a change from Producer Capitalism to Finance Capitalism - leading to more unemployment – a sheer waste of an important factor of production. If at all, the growth of 'credit' and consequently the money supply has to be curtailed, it would be a better and cost effective method to raise 'reserve' requirements against bank's current accounts, which would limit credit growth without increasing the cost for the economy overall.

(iii) **Restrain budget deficits with an ultimate goal for a balanced budget** : By setting targets in the realm of budget proposals, the WB / IMF couple practically takeover the reins of economy and its management, leaving the government in the role of 'faithful implementers' without the ability to question the merits of various propositions and facing the populace and the 'sovereign parliament' as zombies. In its desire to see budget deficits curtailed, it imposes harsh conditionalities, such as:

(i)   reduce and ultimately eliminate official subsidies except for the export sector (Attention Reader: Note the latter for the benefit accruing to the importing west)

(ii)   privatize all state industries, allowing free play for market forces to determine prices of related products and services

(iii)   Introduce de-regulations, in all spheres of activities, leaving the markets to self regulate with a very non-intrusive supervisory role for the government.

(iv)   Shift taxation policy from progressive (direct) to regressive (indirect) taxation – GST and the like and continue to increase latter progressively.

(v)   Open local market to foreign suppliers by reducing import duties under the WTO/Globalization scheme of things

The cumulative effect of the aforesaid policy prescription is that Pakistan's economy is in tatters with both domestic and international debt rising steeply. The most worrying aspect is that of the international debt outstanding at about US$ 60 billion which has witnessed a sharp increase in the last 2/3 years. The foreign lenders particularly the IMF / WB / ADB, have appeared very accommodating in extending loan facilities, at every beck and call of Pakistani government; what is most questionable, however, is the premise or basis on which these organizations have assessed the viability of their lendings to Pakistan. Undoubtedly, no lender will lend money unless he is quite sure of the capacity of the borrower to repay according to the terms and conditions negotiated for the proposed loan facility. With Pakistan's Trading & Current accounts, of its Balance of Payments in perpetual deficits (save some unique exception for a year or two), how do these institutions assume repayments, according to terms agreed, from this primary source. Long term (FDI) foreign direct investments into Pakistan are hardly sufficient to fund these repayments on a regular basis. Although the 'devaluation' factor has further negatively affected the budget expenditures, this, of its own, will not generate foreign currency funds needed for repayment. And if it is a presumption that the local currency counterpart funds of the outstanding repayment liability of foreign currencies, howsoever generated, will be applied by selling these (rupee funds) against purchases of foreign currency in the market, there can be no greater fallacy despite all the talk of the Pakistani rupee's convertibility on Current & Capital Accounts. On the other hand, if we are to believe the latter, then there is no need to borrow in foreign exchange; rather our requirements of the same can be met by outright purchases in foreign exchange markets against rupee sales without attracting humiliating 'conditionalities'. So despite all the mess up the 'devaluation' factor has created for the economy, and given the inability of other avenues of the economy in generating foreign exchange, there is no possibility of meeting repayment obligations, in foreign currency other than borrowing more of the same, camouflaged as 'balance of payment' support, inter alia, for building foreign exchange reserves with corresponding increases in external debt liabilities. At each such instance, even more harsh terms are negotiated by way of 'conditionalities' for the so called 'Standby Arrangements' of IMF, which Mr. Joseph Gold of the legal department of IMF informs us are not mentioned in the original Articles of the Fund or even in the amendments that became effective on July 28 1969. What then is the 'legal' standing of these 'Standby Arrangements' of IMF and its 'conditionalities', which have caused nations in the developing world to lose their economic sovereignty at the altar of IMF?

Devaluation, in its own right, is one of the major factors contributing to inflation where imports are insensitive to price changes – inelastic, so to speak. And in Pakistan the demand for imports generally is inelastic – e.g. petroleum products, palm oil etc.

Privatization, particularly of the utilities in energy sector, with monopolistic power, have created an absolute hell for the general public and enterprises by raising prices with the sole motive of profit maximization, which, by circular process, have increased unit cost of product and services leading to an upward movement in general price – level / inflation.

De-regulation in the financial sector has led to higher costs and rising debts, with banking sector's profitability rising to astronomical levels leading to higher dividend payouts to overseas share holders which, in effect, puts even more strain on Pakistan's scarce foreign exchange resources, when such dividends are converted in foreign currency for remittance abroad.

With respect to 'reforms' in the capital markets, speculative versus genuine equity participation in new or existing projects has broken all records so much so that whilst world capital markets may, at times, be displaying weaknesses, the Karachi Stock Exchange keeps its upward trend despite poor economic fundamentals and then 'they' say the share price index is a reflection or a barometer of the economy! In reality, it is the demonstration of a pure CASINO in operation. With no social security net available to the general public, withdrawal of subsidies have a telling effect on the poor majority [Pakistan's 60 percent population lives at or below poverty level] and then this 'reform' is marketed under 'poverty elimination' prescription of these humane world lending agencies, all in pursuit of 'human rights' of which the West is the undoubted champion of the world.

Not content with heaping such gross miseries on the simple folks, there comes another bombshell in the form of regressive taxation GST etc which is totally unmindful of the financial capacity of different classes of people to pay such taxes, at flat rates, across the board.

By thrusting WTO/globalization policies (as part of the 'conditionalities') down the country's throat, forcing the economy to open up to foreign suppliers of goods by reducing import duties / barriers, the local industry begins to shut down on account of cheaper competition from abroad [foreign firms have an advantage of low energy cost, low borrowing cost, higher technology and economies of scale in their production activities] leading to increasing unemployment and resultant aggravation of base poverty. One may question, how an economy in such financial straits, as is the case with Pakistan, support imports of practically everything under the sun? Of course, why not? We have fabulous 'reserves' which are so eagerly funded by our well wishers headquartered in Washington D.C. (read letters D.C. for Devil's Capital) by loan after loan totally devoid of the 'bankability' of such financial propositions.

It may come as a surprise to many that according to research conducted by many independent consultants / scholars, the developing world continues to be saddled with huge international indebtedness [in monetary / financial terms] yet the fact is that, through the process of devaluations of their local currencies, these countries have repaid their indebtedness many times over in physical transfer of real wealth i.e. their produce, to their creditor's nations at exceptionally low prices – a transfer of resources from the poor to the rich. Now you see the miracle of 'devaluation' and why policy prescriptions of these lending agencies begin with emphasis on exchange rate adjustments.

To reclaim economic sovereignty, it is of critical importance that the issue of external debt be addressed not in the paradigm of 'sustainability of debt' but in a policy prescription requiring its substantial liquidation, so that the 'conditionalities' that accompany such debts are done away with, and the economy is able to move forward in keeping with domestic ground realities.

In doing so, the balance of payment needs to be the target of prime importance, for this should be the source that is to fund repayments of foreign currency debt obligations and in a way, so to speak, should act as a parallel and independent money supply denominated in foreign currency. To give effect, a separate 'budget' denominated in foreign currency needs to be in place which should progressively aim to reduce aggregate deficits moving to an ideal of a 'balanced' foreign currency budget over time. Imports needs to be controlled and the exchange rate needs to be managed more in the context of fixed exchange rate regime rather than allowing it to sink perpetually. For devaluation implies transfer of greater volumes of real resources, at low prices, against inadequate financial inflows of foreign exchange, which are insufficient to service the debt.

As an illustration of the 'devaluation factor', a simple example will elaborate the issue:

Pakistan, let us assume, exports ten units of product A @ US$ 100 per unit at an exchange rate of Rs.50 per US$. This results in gross income of US$ 1000 which in terms of rupees yields Rs.50,000 at the exchange rate of Rs.50/$.

Now, let us assume the rupee is devalued and the new exchange rate is Rs.100 per US$ 1. With no change in the quantity sold and the price per unit charged, the exporter's new gross income would remain unchanged i.e. US$ 1000 but he would now realize Rs.100,000, a 100% increase in local currency. The importer realizing this change in the exchange rate and assuming that no additional local cost has been incurred by the exporter in the production of this product A, would demand equal, proportionate, price reduction of Product A. Let us assume the exporter agrees. This in effect will call upon him to now export 10 units of product A @US$ 50 per unit, realizing for him US$ 500, giving him Rs.50,000 @ Rs.100 per $ 1 as before. Whilst in terms of dollar inflow (financial flow) there has been a net reduction of $ 500; in rupee terms exporter's income remains unaffected at Rs.50,000/-. The effect of devaluation therefore has had a beneficial effect on the importer, that he now buys the same quantity of Product A but at half the original price, which correspondingly reduces the net foreign exchange inflow for Pakistan from $ 1000 to $ 500. How is it then assumed that with perpetual devaluations of Rupee, Pakistan will ever be in a position to meet / liquidate its foreign currency debt obligations with reducing financial inflows of foreign exchange against constant export volumes? Another alternative, to make up the loss in foreign exchange inflows is to increase volumes — this in effect substantiates the claim that devaluation results in transfer of real resources from poor countries to rich countries at low cost, with confirmation that under this scenario, foreign currency debt obligations of developing world towards the Industrialized West have been repaid many times over, in terms of real wealth transferred as against debt obligations outstanding in monetary terms.

The other proposed positive effect of devaluation, that is to bring about a fundamental change in trading account from deficit to surplus, has proved false in the 30 year history of Pakistani Rupee devaluation; from 1982 to date.

To SUMMARIZE, Pakistan needs to reorient its economic policy, in its international trading sphere, by putting in place a mechanism for the preparation of a foreign currency budget, effectively indicating how it proposes to reduce its international debt obligations in aggregate over time supported by an effective exchange rate policy with greater emphasis of its management to near fixed exchange regime, control on imports, invoicing of trade in the currencies of its trading partners, on bilateral basis, rather than US Dollar exclusively, so that the 'conditionalties' of the

INTERNATIONAL MONEY LORDS may be bade good bye for ever – a pipe dream perhaps but certainly worth a try!

Chapter IV

Islamic Banking

"The devil himself can cite scripture for his own purpose."

Karl Marx.

It is an irony of fate that Islamic Banking came to be introduced in the 'Land of the Pure', where angels fear to tread, upon the alleged judicial murder of its first elected Prime Minister during the reign of His Holiness – General Zia-ul-Haq, the Amir ul Momineen, to stalk the land of the born-again Muslims.

In the dispensation of Islamic Banking, all public deposits accepted by the banking sector are on the basis of 'Profit and loss sharing' – implying a relationship between customer and bank that of Investor and Investee; yet no banking related legislation, formally amending the conventional 'debtor / credit' relationship between customer and bank, has been introduced.

Notwithstanding, current accounts are an exception to the aforesaid practice, which are accepted as 'loans' from the depositor, repayable on demand with discretion available with the banker as to its use and income thereof to which current account depositor has no right of claim and / or enquiry as to its deployment.

Current and Saving accounts are both 'cheque book' based accounts where savings accounts are generally operated as current accounts except for large amount withdrawals where notice period condition may be enforced. Savings accounts have a minimum 5% pa payout, as profit, as decreed by State Bank which is normally accrued monthly, on minimum monthly balance basis.

Placement of deposits on profit & loss sharing basis may have some adverse consequences for the depositors, which, regrettably, banking institutions do not highlight for information of the general public-potential depositors.

These are:

(i)   that the principal sum deposited is also at risk in the event of losses on investments which the banker will undertake on behalf of the depositor / investor but at banker's sole discretion without assuming any risk for itself whatsoever unless wilful negligence / fraud is proved against the banker.

(ii)   The rate of profit is subject to change, at banker's discretion, during the tenor of the placement from the indicative rate advised at the time of placement of deposit. Generally however, and as per practice, the indicative rate holds for the duration of deposit placement but can change, should circumstances so demand, which the depositor will have to accept as part of the terms and conditions of the profit and loss sharing provisions of the relative deposit scheme.

(iii)   The 'profits' of the bank that is eligible for sharing with the depositor / investor is limited to gross income accruing to the bank from its financing activities on 'markup' basis and other modes of Islamic financing engaged into and not other income that accrues to the bank, in addition, from other sources of revenue. Whilst this may, in effect, give a lower rate of profit for the depositor / investor, its benefit, to the depositor / investor, on the other hand is when the banker is running a net loss on his profit and loss position and yet the depositor / investor gets a positive return as long as there is a net positive spread between income earned from activities relating to Islamic modes of financing and expenses to be met, by profit distributions, on deposits.

The mechanics of profit distribution is slightly different with banks exclusively incorporated as Islamic Banks, whose financing and investment activities are wholly based on Islamic modes of financings, save the current accounts which are operated at par with conventional banking practices.

In Islamic Banks, all deposits, save current account, are pooled which are then deployed in Assets Backed Financing, Investments and Placements, a sizeable portion of investments being deployed in Government of Pakistan Ijarah Sukuks (in place of Treasury bills) which are backed by Government of Pakistan sovereign guarantee yielding profits generally based on 6 months weighted average yield of six months market T-bill plus a fixed margin. Gross income so derived for the pool, is distributed in the ratio of 60:40 (after netting expenses directly attributable to pool and profit distributed to other special pools) between the depositor and the bank, where the latter's share represents his fee as Investment Manager, in which role he invests the 'pool' funds at his discretion but at the sole risk of the depositor / investor who assumes all the risks. The bank, however, is a 'pool' participant with respect to bank's equity, which, strictly speaking, appears as unfunded book entry in the books of the bank. On this, the bank shares, appropriately, in the profit available to 'pool' participants. A fairly lucrative, risk free source of income for the investment manager.

In the case of Pakistan's leading Islamic bank, profit after taxation increased from Rs.223 million in 2002 to Rs.1.649 billion in 2010.

Generally, the profit rate paid to depositors and the financing cost charged to borrowers under Islamic banks are not at great variance from those of the conventional commercial banks. Had this been so, a discernable shift of business from conventional to Islamic banks would have been witnessed. Islamic banks, however, have 'hair splitting' documentation enforced under the guideline of their Shariah Supervisory Boards and advisors, who have, somehow, to justify their presence and role.

The banking sector, both in the conventional and Islamic characteristics is functioning giving the comfort to the depositors that their incomes derived from placements with banks are legitimate (halal) in the context of prohibition on interest (riba), for, as they claim, these are 'profits' and not 'interest' – the former fluctuation based whilst the latter based on a fixed, predetermined rate.

Notwithstanding this in the words of a researcher, the implementation mechanism *"indicates clearly that the prohibition of RIBA has little practical (effect) in that the doctors of the law demonstrated great ingenuity in finding ways of getting around the theoretical prohibition. .... Hanafite School (to which al-kassaf and shaybani belonged) was the most tolerant, (in history) applying to this case its principle that necessity renders legitimate that which, strictly speaking, is forbidden"* – *Islam & Capitalism (Maxime Rodinson).* And, of course, the Land of the Pure is past master when it comes to implementation of the *LAW OF NECESSITY*.

The aforesaid quotation is very meaningful in the context that for both conventional and Islamic banks, *the current and saving accounts, backed by cheque books, are the principal source of the 'deception' that banker engages in, when he creates money out of thin air* – as explained in Chapter-I. And the aggregate sums invested / deposited under these heads represents the major share of aggregate deposits of a banking house generally.

The Supreme Court of Pakistan (Shariat Appellate Jurisdiction) in M. Aslam Khaki V Muhammad Hashim – PLD 2000 SC 225 had examined the issue of RIBA in great detail and pronounced its historic judgment only to confront yet another soldier of fortune at the helm of affairs in whose reign the verdict was not allowed its sway but instead, on an appeal from United Bank Limited – public sector organization at the time, was put in cold storage by asking Council of Islamic Ideology to re-visit the issue of Riba which they have not done to date and quite rightly so, because this reconsideration was not genuinely intended but was merely an exercise in delaying the issue indefinitely. Don't you, dear reader, marvel at this and the Pure and the born – again Muslims of Pakistan!!.

Well, just for the record, I quote from the judgment a few of the pronouncements of the Learned and Honourable Lordships, who sat on the bench to hear this case.

On the markup mode of financing:

> *"Evidently, the objective behind some of the affirmative observations, regarding the mark-up system is merely to sanction trading, upon duly and fully complying with the concepts of Bai – Mu'ajjal and Marabaha sale, each observing the caution, administered by the Holy Prophet (s.a.a.ws) of physical delivery of goods sold."*
>
> *Justice Wajiuddin Ahmed - Member*

On prohibition w.r.t. Islamic History:

> *"History testifies the prohibition to have been so well-delineated and clearly understood that trade or commercial transactions amongst Muslims, for the best past of the ensuing fourteen hundred years of the Islamic era, have essentially remained free of all taints of interest or riba. Whenever deviations took place, and those occurred largely at the level of Muslim Rulers, the transgressors had to pay heavily not only in economic but also in practical terms. In point is the example of the Ottoman Caliphate, which, in large measure, owes its disintegration to international debt".*
>
> *Justice Wajiuddin Ahmed - Member*

About bank account:

> *"Thus, we are left only with the last option, namely, that bank accounts are investments within the meaning of Ra's al'Mal of a Mudarabah or Musharkah".*

"The principal of AMANAT (account) requires that AMIN should only protect and keep it in safe custody and should only protect and should have no authority to dispose of that money".

Justice Khalil-ur-Rehman-Chairman

About mark-up as originally envisaged by the council of Islamic Ideology

"The council of Islamic Ideology in its report on the 'Elimination of interest' had approved the use of the mark-up system, Bai Mu'ajjal, to a limited extent in unavoidable cases in the process of switching over to an interest-free system and warned against its wide or indiscriminate use in view of the danger attached to it viz opening of a back door for dealings on the basis of interest. It is unfortunate that this warning was not properly heeded and the system of markup adopted in January, 1981 did not conform to the standard stipulation of Bai Mu'ajjal".

Justice Khalil ur Rehman – Chairman.

In view of the foregoing observations and the general practices of the interest-free / Islamic banking, it would not be wrong to say that the current banking practices in Pakistan, with respect to deposit taking and lending, remain unchanged in essence; 'profit' replacing the word 'interest' without any meaningful change in substance, courtesy our learned scholars bedecking the Shariah Boards with their skills displayed in coming up with documentation to sanctify illegal nature of the transaction, in the Islamic context.

To SUMMARIZE then, the so-called interest free / Islamic banking that is in operation is in reality a 'make believe' exercise where the 'deceptive' role of banker, in creating money out of nothing, through the 'fractional reserve banking' continues unabated. To cater to the zeal of the 'born-again' Muslims, a change in nomenclature has been made but at a serious disadvantage of the prospective banking customers who have been saddled with greater risks, low returns on their deposits and higher cost on their borrowings than before. In return banker's net income has gone through the roof, with the regulator content to allow the market free play with no role to supervise the mechanics in the determination of rates of return to the depositors, which are in effect 'negative' vis-à-vis the current inflation rate.

Chapter V

Euro-Currency Market

"We are grateful to the Washington Post, the New York Times, Time Magazine and other great publications whose directors have attended our meetings and respected their promise of discretion for almost forty years. It would have been impossible for us to develop our plan for the world if we had been subjected to the lights of publicity during those years. But the world is now more sophisticated and prepared to march towards a world government. The supra national sovereignty of an intellectual elite and world bankers is surely preferable to the national auto-determination practiced in past centuries."

David Rockefeller

Monetary policy, a select preserve of a nation's central bank, is concerned with the principal task of maintaining price stability, in an economy, through the mechanism of money supply by attempting to ensure, prima facie, that money, the neutral medium of exchange, should be sufficient to facilitate exchange in goods and services that an economy produces. Money, in its own right, will not sustain human life in the absence of goods and services, for if there is nothing to exchange, money will be useless as an exchange medium.

Management of conventional monetary policy, in the context of money supply, entails increase / decrease of interest rate to control demand for money; institution of Cash Reserves requirements, to limit the multiplying factor of the 'Fractional Reserve Banking System'; open money market operations of the central bank, to withdraw or supply money as deemed appropriate and selective credit control to dictate flow of funds to specific areas of activities in keeping with national priorities.

What is the ideal level of quantity of money that is budgeted annually for a particular economy, is left at the sole discretion of the monetary authorities, who decide the level of 'Credit' growth the economy has to undergo for the period projected in keeping with the prime goal of maintaining price stability.

The Fractional Reserve Banking, being the principal tool for the creation of money, by the banking system, is limited in scope with regard to the 'cash reserve' that banking institutions are required to maintain as part of the monetary policy. For the 'Money Lords' this limiting factor and other controlling tools of the monetary authorities were inhibiting their urge to be the complete masters of money without any outside restrain on their monopolistic powers. Hence came into existence the EURO DOLLAR market, more precisely the EURO CURRENCY MARKET.

The aforesaid monetary system from the time of the end of World War II uptill August 15, 1971 was structured on the following premises as part of the Bretton Woods Agreements, with IMF entrusted with responsibility to ensure exchange rate stability on world wide basis and facilitate international trade in an orderly fashion.

1) Fixed exchange rate regimes with defined parities, allowing free movement of exchange rate within a band of 1% above and 1% below the given parities against US Dollars, for trading activities, impacting current accounts called TRADE FLOWS.

2) Fluctuating exchange rate mechanism for transactions of capital nature, impacting capital account called FINANCIAL FLOWS and subject to local exchange

control regulations – for instance, in UK, the Investment Currency Pool; in USA, Regulation Q of the Federal Reserve Bank; in Continental Europe, financial exchange rate which was at a premium vis-à-vis the commercial exchange rate, latter for trade / commercial transactions.

3) To assist nations with temporary balance of payment difficulties, with supply of international convertible currencies, in cash. Where, however, such deficits persisted overtime, about 3 year or more, leading to a situation of 'Fundamental disequilibrium' in their respective balance of payments, emphasis was laid on deficit prone countries, to devalue their currencies rather than burdening the surplus countries with corrective revaluation of their currencies in accordance with policy adopted by IMF, in 1944 / 45, on the recommendation of HARRY DEXTER – US representative, as opposed to KEYNES suggestion for an International Currency clearing union, for the remedy of international financial imbalance of trade. Countries refusing to follow IMF recommendation for devaluation were threatened with having their currency declared SCARCE CURRENCY with serious adverse consequences in their international trading activities.

4) The monetization of gold held as 'reserve' by the Central banks @ US$ 35 per oz of fine gold, at which rate US Dollar was convertible in gold for all non-US residents.

These policy prescriptions worked quite well uptill about 1965 or so, where international liquidity was supporting upto 90% of Trade flows and 10% of capital flows. In the environment of limiting gold supply to meet growing requirements of international liquidity, countries whose currencies were deemed international reserve currencies, particularly Britain were compelled to supply international liquidity instead, by running deficits on their balance of payments, which, in the case of Britain, appeared to be adversely affecting its own economic health.

This led USA to slowly step in from 1965 onwards, on an ever increasing scale, as the world's principal reserve currency provider. Notwithstanding, a raging debate ensued in the west focusing on the inadequacy of international reserves, which IMF, in particular, tried to meet by introducing special Drawing Rights issue, on the pattern of BANCOR originally proposed by Keynes. This, however, did not stem the international outcry for reforms with respect to exchange rate regime, gold parity and exchange control regulations to supplement international liquidity for meeting growing international trade requirements, growth of which was said to be outstripping the supply of international reserve and hence international liquidity.

During the period, a money market called The Euro Currency Market had quietly come into existence. To be precise, it made its humble beginnings in around 1950s, beginning to impact the international money market in 1957 / 58. *"It arrived on the market without credentials either from the IMF or from any other international institution. It is now recognized as the first SUPRANATIONAL money market. It is unfettered by the rules & restrictions of any national authorities. Its emergence has been wisely criticized as some kind of conspiracy against governments and especially against the United States. There is a grain of truth in the argument." The Euro dollar Market – Werner M.M. Makowski.*

The Market is normally called the Eurodollar Market given that the US Dollar share in the market is around 80%. Its rationale lay in the fact that Soviet Union and its East European satellite states, during the cold war era, had substantial inflows of foreign exchange denominated in US Dollar. These states had the option to convert these US Dollar inflows into other convertible currency or else hold them on deposit with US banking system till their utilization. Given the nature of cold war relationship, particularly between USSR and USA, the Soviets did not feel comfortable in placing their US Dollars on deposit in USA fearing their forfeiture in the event of their political relationship moving towards hostility. And, they were also not inclined to seek US Dollars conversion in other convertible currencies on account of the fact that oil imports from Middle East had to be paid for in US Dollars, being the only currency of invoicing of oil world wide. Conversion into other currencies, in the first instance and its reconversion later into US Dollars, to make oil payments, would have entailed a substantial exchange risk exposure and cost for the Soviets and its allies. Consequently, a via media was found where the US Dollars were placed, on deposit, with British banks (Britain having a much more reliable record in honoring its financial obligations notwithstanding political irritants in its international relations with other countries) in the name of USSR and its entities. The UK banks, in turn placed the deposit with US bank in its name, in Nostro Accounts, by cash, wire transfer. The deposits with British banks were basically 'off balance sheet' transaction in so far as UK financial authorities / regulators were concerned and were not subject to any UK regulatory supervision and / or regulator's liquidity cash requirements etc. These deposits came to acquire the nomenclature of 'Eurodollars' being US dollar deposits outside the financial jurisdiction of the US banking regulators. As explained earlier, in Chapter-I, the word 'deposit' is technically a misnomer; for in fact these are 'loans' extended by the depositors under the 'debtor / creditor' relationship. The British bank while placing the deposits onwards with the US banking houses had also a concurrent ability to lend the amount

appearing in their books as dollar deposit, in full, to prospective
borrower making a call on the British bank on non-cash basis, by
internal book transfer entries, on a pattern similar to 'fractional reserve
banking' system. Why is it that in this market, the 'full' amount of
deposit can be lent out? The reason being, that since 'Eurodollar'
market is not subject to national regulator's rules and regulations, there
are no 'cash liquidity / reserve requirements' to be met and hence the
'full' amount is available for lending, if the bank so desires.
Theoretically, such 'Euro dollar' deposits can be multiplied, through
the process of deposit taking and lending ad-infinitum, as opposed to
'fractional reserve banking' system where the process of multiplication
is factored on the given cash reserve / liquidity requirement imposed
by the national banking regulators. *"It is one of the paradoxes of
modern banking that it enables us to eat our cake and keep it.
The same dollars which are lent abroad by their foreign owners
can be used simultaneously by American banks for lending to the
United States or abroad. The result of a transfer of a deposit to
the Eurodollar market is that the volume of dollars lent by non-
American banks increases without corresponding reduction in
the volume of dollars lent by the American banks. This means
the increase in the grand total of the international volume of
credit resources".* The Euro Dollar System – Paul Einzig.

This source of creating unlimited international liquidity, solely at private banking initiative, with no control over its activities by national banking regulators, has led to massive speculations in commodities, futures market, gold, mergers, and takeovers and at defeating national monetary policies particularly in initiatives at controlling credit growth impacting domestic money supply. Today, it is estimated that international liquidity is supporting 'financial flows' to the extent of 90% and 'Trade Flows' to the extent of 10%. No national financial authority can determine the size of this market and hence all domestic monetary policies of the industrialized countries are at the mercy of this market. It is said, ***"Only under a World Government could there be an effective international monetary policy. But the effort of the B.I.S. (Bank for International Settlement) to influence the Euro-Dollar market is a step in that direction"*** *Paul Einzig.*

And of course, what is this B.I.S.?

The Bank for International Settlements – B.I.S. in an international clearing house; a supranational organization for setting and implementing global monetary strategy, THE BANK of the leading centrals banks of the world; and is not accountable to any national government. It works closely with IMF and the Federal Reserve Bank of USA.

The Euro-dollar market has formally no lender of last resort, for it operates outside the financial jurisdiction of national regulators; it has, however since 1967, been a recipient of official intervention in the form of lending by the BIS, who is known to employ large funds in this market for its own account and for the accounts of its various member central banks. *Between the Eurodollar market & BIS, you have 'the supranational sovereignty of world bankers' – the world's MONEY LORDS, who have total, undisputed monopoly power over all money so created by the process of 'debt'.*

"*In order to mitigate the effects of American borrowing on interest rates, the B.I.S. increased the extent of its intervention in the Eurodollar market during 1967. It lent Euro dollars on a large scale, partly with aid of Euro dollars which many central banks were anxious to lend for the sake of the tempting yield, but largely through acquiring dollars from the Federal Reserve for the purpose. To that end it made increased use of its swap arrangements with the Federal Reserve. To a very large extent the dollars lent by the B.I.S. to the Euro-dollar market were provided by the Federal Reserve. A vicious cycle thus came to be created. Dollars borrowed by American banks from the Euro dollar market were re-lent by Federal Reserve to the Euro dollar market through the intermediary of the B.I.S. The resulting increase in the supply of Euro-dollars to be precise, the replacement of supplies borrowed by American banks – enabled American banks to borrow even more" – Paul Einzig.*

The unhindered power of the Euro-dollar market to create unlimited US Dollars outside the financial borders of USA has a unique feature in the context of US money supply. These additional dollars are not reflected in the US Money Supply; save the comparatively nominal amounts transferred to USA via the cash wire transfers and its multiplication within the US economy by the process of fractional reserve banking. To hide this aspect the US Federal Reserve, since 2006, has abolished publication of the broadest money supply aggregate M3. Whilst the currency of the world's largest economy gets issued at the sole discretion of private bankers, within and without, there is no central national mechanism to determine its aggregate total, issued and outstanding. Under the circumstances, how can USA run an effective national monetary policy or for that matter other leading world economies, given that their currencies too are subject to uncontrolled creation by private financial powers exercising their authority outside the financial borders of these countries. Rather than making a concerted effort to effectively block this unlimited creation of their currencies through the Eurocurrency market; USA, Japan, Germany and other leading lights of the industrialized West have borrowed extensively through this market – USA financing its

Vietnam adventure through this market leading to enormous amounts of dollars coming in the hands of foreign government, as reserves, and enterprises as income / surpluses – labeled in Europe around early 1970s as the era of a 'dollar overhang'.

It is this dollar 'overhang' which prompted France, in 1971, to call the US bluff on the issue of convertibility of dollar into gold @ $35 per oz. of gold. It began to formally demand gold against sales of US dollars at the stated price, asking US to physically transfer the due quantities of gold to France. US complied initially, but later restricted such dollar sales with a view to convertibility into gold, to French dollar holdings as reserves and surpluses with French state sector. Seeing the demand persisting, US authorities forbade physical transfers of gold to France but instead allowed transfer within the four walls of Fort Knox [US gold vault] from one room to another, latter bearing the name plate 'Property of the Republic of France'. Undeterred French demand continued until, on August 15, 1971, President Nixon announced the suspension of the dollar convertibility into gold at the fixed price of US$ 42 per oz of gold – the dollar having recently been devalued in terms of gold by 10 percent – realizing the insufficiency of gold to back the total issue of US dollars issued and outstanding.

This marked the end of the era of monetized gold at the stated fixed price leading US dollar and correspondingly all other international convertible currencies of the world to the status of 'fiat' money without commodity backing. World monetary authorities followed this act by succumbing to vested interest demand for adopting the 'floating' exchange rate regimes, in place of 'fixed' exchange rate regimes. Technically, IMF's principal role of managing the fixed exchange rate system on the backing of monetized gold at a fixed rate, thus came to an end.

Money growth, fueling international liquidity, surpassed the most optimistic estimates ultimately leading to a multiple of 4 to world's GDP resulting in huge speculative capital flows across the world meeting its Waterloo in the collapse and the meltdown of Western World's Financial System in 2008 / 09 with USA in the lead. *A substitute Financial System, as part of the anticipated World Government, was being nursed all along by the Money Lords who now have in place the Eurocurrency money market and the Bank for International Settlement, latter as the central bank for the one world setup, the intellectual leadership of which is being provided by the ultra secretive organization called the Bilderberg Group* [For a detailed account of this group, see 'The true story of Bilderberg group' by Daniel Estulin].

To SUMMARIZE, the world financial set up, put in place as a consequence of Bretton Woods agreements, with IMF in the lead, to supervise fixed exchange rate mechanism and monetization of gold at fixed rate, has now ceased to exist; yet IMF continues to exist, interfering in national domestic financial policies, with ulterior motive to dismantle the welfare oriented economies of the West by recommending austerity measures to control budget deficits and government's aggregate debt. For the lesser developed world, IMF policy prescriptions are even worst in exacerbating the poverty levels in these countries without offering any meaningful remedies for improving the lot of the majority. ***Since the whole world economy is debt based, where money comes into existence through debt rather than through savings,*** it would be self-contradictory for IMF to effectively reduce World's aggregate debts outstanding for such a policy would adversely affect the 'Money Lords' who have fabulous source of income, as interest on debt, which they create out of thin air with control over practically all the assets of the world as collateral for debt.

Fiscal and Money policies of the governments of industrialized West are at the mercy of supranational financial institutions over which they have no control. Every where the outstanding debts are merely rolled over at new terms, to apparently soften the impact of interest payments but offsetting the same with harsh conditions which otherwise mitigate against the well being of its people. It remains to be seen whether the West will take steps to be the master of its destiny or will subject itself to the one world government where 'Money Lords' will rule with impunity!

Chapter VI

Inflation

"Nature .... proceeded to work out and to inflict on her human subjects the inequitable consequences of such 'get-rich-quick' maneuvers. Those consequences were economic misery".

Professor Irving Fisher.

Maintenance of price stability is the avid goal of monetary policy and all its tools are employed to manage money supply so that the classical inflation 'too much money chasing too few goods' or conversely 'too many goods chasing less money' latter leading to deflation, is avoided. Given that money creation is almost all debt based, it is, in effect, too much 'debt' money that is primarily responsible for aggravating the price stability in an economy, causing rise in price level or, in common parlance, creating inflation.

Inflation itself can be classified either as DEMAND PULL or COST PUSH. Historical evidence points out to the fact that *'abundance & scarcity of goods have never substantially moved the price level' – Fisher* – rather it has been shortage or excess of the circulating medium – Money – that has been the principal cause of the movement of price levels; to be precise a case of 'monetary inflation', that is, Cost Push in current economic terminology.

The 'demand pull' aspect is primarily related to *"supply / demand equation of goods, where miscellaneous factors act separately on a miscellany of separate goods, only seldom joining in any great concerted up-influence or down – influence. Money, on the other hand, must tend to affect all prices alike. In this moving or affecting all prices in concert, the tide of money does not in the least interfere with the relative ups and downs of individual prices. The individual prices are still subject to enlargement or concentration by separate influences operating within the various inconsistent supplies & demands, but the scale of the whole assortment of motions enlarges or diminishes as the money tide swells or ebbs" – INFLATION by Professor Irving Fisher.*

To illustrate the foregoing, Fisher supports his arguments by a graphic presentation of prices of wheat in silver (one kind of money) for 2500 years.

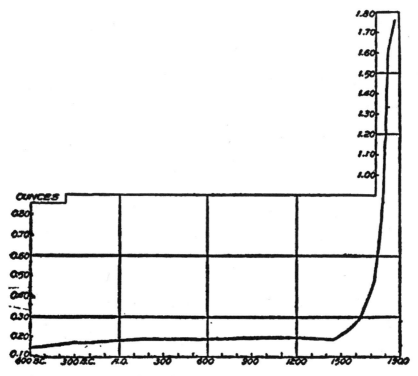

Chart 4. Prices of Wheat in Silver for 2500 Years.

He states, *"the point to be noted is that, after the discovery of America, the price of wheat shot up like a sky rocket (a four hundred year sky-rocket), concurring with a silver – supply sky-rocket, and not in the least concurring with either wheat production or wheat demand. These production-demand factors are not recorded in the chart, but history records quite sufficiently that the production of wheat did not dwindle in these sky-rocket years. On the contrary, the two Americas were constantly adding to the production, and this would tend to lower the price of wheat-not raise it. Nor did the* demand *for wheat* increase; *on the contrary, substitutes for wheat were continually entering into competition with it, thus further tending to lower the price of it; so that the chief demand factors and the chief supply factors would* both *tend to lower the price of wheat, not raise it. What did raise it, then, century after century, in terms of silver? Of course, it was the silver itself, which started inflating after the discovery of America".*

Accordingly, it is the monetary inflation / deflation that is the bone of contention and so long as money creation, by the process of debt, remains vested in the private hands who have the power to increase or decrease its supply, at will, price stability will remain a far cry. It is therefore, of critical importance for the national authorities to first determine the volume of circulating medium-money-a neutral medium of exchange – proportionate to the level of goods and services being produced by an economy so that it moves in parallel with GDP. Ideally, the money supply – M2 should be equal to GDP monetized. This will, in effect, facilitate price stability; price level approaching a constant level.

To quote Fisher again, *"the goods should increase PER CAPITA and the money should follow suit – increasing PER CAPITA but neither increasing nor decreasing PER GOODS. Real inflation and deflation are inflation / deflation PER GOODS; and the weekly test of whether the goods and the circulation are in step is the index number of prices. The price level almost invariably shifts the MONETARY FACTORS – gold, silver, paper, credit – and very little with COMMODITY factors. The latter control only the deviations of individual prices from the average price movement. In a word, supply and demand dictate each individual price RELATIVE TO PRICE LEVEL, BUT MONEY DICTATES PRICE LEVEL ITSELF. So much for money as a cause, and the price level as an EFFECT"*. Fisher laments at our technicians who are responsible for our money by saying that they have yet to see the cause though they see the effect, rather vaguely.

In view of the foregoing, it would be appropriate now to address the expert opinions aired in the electronic and print media as to the issue of inflation, reflected in price increase across the board which is the issue hotly debated in the field of economics. The question principally engaged in during the panel discussions and / or column contributed by educated elites from their Ivory Castles is the act of the government in funding its rising expenditures by printing of currency notes – legal tender-through 'borrowings' from the central bank, State Bank, which is claimed by all and sundry, IMF included, to be highly inflationary. The fallacy of this argument would become apparent, prima-facie, when the train of events are examined in sequence. This we will do presently:

- It has to be borne in mind that the Government (GOP) is 'borrowing' from another body – corporate or otherwise.

- For the lender to lend, it must have 'surplus' from which to lend, which is, of course, common sense, for nobody lends unless he has something to lend.

- Does State Bank have such surplus funds to lend?

- If State Bank is going through its ISSUE DEPARTMENT, the answer is that it has no surplus funds to lend from this source.

- To raise funds or more precisely to issue additional currency notes, to meet GOP's demand, State Bank approaches the printing press to do so, against the security of government's IOUs, called market Treasury bills, bearing interest, which the government had earlier got printed through the same printing press.

- Alternatively, State Bank can seek to raise the required funds proceeding through its BANKING DEPARTMENT, auctioning the Treasury Bills to the banking system inviting bids. For the acceptable bid, State Bank will exchange these bills against payment received from the buying banks.

- In both the cases, a national debt has come into existence for the amounts borrowed, on which the state / government pays interest, in the case of former, to State Bank and in the latter, to the buying banks.

- Funding the government through printing of notes is said to be inflationary whereas seeking funds from banking system against sales of Treasury bill is not, because note printing is said to be a creation out of nothing whilst obtaining funds from the banking system is said to be a transfer payment, being funded from deposits which, so it is claimed, are public savings in origination.

- As earlier explained in Chapter-I, money creation by the banking system is largely money created out of nothing [deposits, except for initial savings in the form of cash injection, are all loans based which are multiplied under fractional reserve banking system]. Therefore both, the note printing and borrowings from the banking system are equally inflationary.

- Once it has been decided that government's increasing expenditures are to be met from borrowings – a given- than the only other consideration is its servicing cost, i.e. interest payment.

- Where the government is empowered to issue Treasury Bills, it should equally be empowered to issue CURRENCY NOTES. The former carries interest liability for the government, in addition to the liability of redemption upon maturity, in favour of the lender, whereas the latter does not, since this involves note issuance by the government itself, without recourse to 'borrowings' thus saving for the government the interest expense and the redemption obligation.

As to the question of 'rising expenditures' of the government, it has to be realized that these have come into existence by way of 'exchange' for the goods and services provided by the economy. In pure barter set up, one set of goods and services provided would be exchanged by a different set of goods and services. But with the introduction of a neutral medium of exchange, in the form of money, the 'exchange' is transmitted via the intermediation of money. As far as GDP is concerned, the additional goods and services provided have already added to its growth and if money is to move in parallel with GDP growth – to avoid the classical deflation of too many goods chasing less money etc addition to money supply by creating additional legal tender is an absolute must. How then is this, in its very simplistic form, inflationary?

Reservations by our economic scholars / intellectuals with regard to printing of currency notes, to meet GOP's immediate funding requirements, is akin to the European 'tranquilizer School' of the late 50's who felt that inflation could be ended quite painlessly by some devise such as limiting the 'note issue' to which the UK's Chancellor of Exchequer responded, *"One does not stop inflation by refusing to print bank notes any more than one cures a fever by trying to hold down the mercury in the thermometer"*.

In SUMMARY, inflation is largely 'monetary' in nature i.e. cost push, avoidance of which will necessitate for the monetary authorities to clearly define the limits of Broad Money Supply to Gross Domestic Product – ideally there should be an equality between the two. Once decided, the limit [in percentage] must be strictly monitored and enforced. The argument that borrowings effected through printing of currency notes are inflationary vis-à-vis borrowings from the banking system, for meeting, in the short term, government's increasing expenditure, over and above the budgeted provisions, is wholly untrue; for money creation from either of the two sources is equally inflationary since, in both cases, it is being created through the thin air, if you please, by a stroke of pen, in the form of a debt. Money supply should ideally follow or be parallel to the increase in goods per capita, to limit the monetary inflationary impact.

Chapter VII

Global Debt Crisis

"A globalized financial system that has delinked the creation of money from the creation of real wealth and rewards extractive over productive investment, (where) speculators capitalize on market volatility to extract a private tax from those engaged in productive work and investment".

When Corporations Rule the World – David C. Konten.

"Let goods be home spun whenever it is reasonably and conveniently possible, and above all, let finance be primarily national".

John Maynard Keynes.

The policy of De-regulation, Free Trade and Unfettered Market Play under the WTO based and corporate led Globalization had finally met its waterloo in the great financial meltdown of 2008/09 to affect the western economies, particularly of the USA and UK.

With personal savings at near zero in these economies, the growth was all debt based, financed principally by US Dollars, mythically created out of thin air by the banking system – domestically and internationally, causing a Tsunami of Dollars world wide.

Corporate America, since early 1980's, took the lead in outsourcing industry by seeking to relocate these to low wage countries causing manufacturing job losses within US compensated by high value employment opportunities in the service industry. This caused *"a shift in the balance of power between corporations & the workers. A pronounced swing in the relative strength of capital versus labour is at the heart of today's financial turbulence". The Credit Crunch-Turner.* Corporations, in pursuit of relentless profits, engaged in over investment and over production overseas. To fund the demand to meet the overproduction, consumer finance was encouraged leading to massive unsecured consumer debt accumulation. A second major avenue of funding consumer spending, on secured basis, was sought by raising finances against owner's equity in the mortgage property – houses, whose prices began to rise on account of easy credit availability by way of second mortgages, leading to a market in sub-prime mortgages.

It was the banker's deception that had led to money creation out of nothing – a water wheel of money creation put into motion effortlessly. To deploy this money in lending operations, to earn interest there from, bankers needed collateral backup. House purchases, through mortgages, were a major lending avenue where a banker would lend, on long term basis, on the security of the house. This was, in essence, a prime lending proposition which would appear on the banker's book for the full duration of the facility. Just as money, created out of nothing, multiplied itself via the fractional reserve banking system, save the initial cash deposit represented by savings, so did the bankers ventured into a similar exercise, in deception, this time of creating artificial collaterals, based on the prime security of the original house by resorting to an unbelievable array of 'Financial Instruments of Mass Destruction'. Now there was plenty of money available for lending and equally plentiful collaterals to support borrowings, albeit in the realm of pure fiction.

We will now examine how the hideously complex financial securities created by turbo charged financial engineering led to the creation of a bloated financial system via the mechanism of cheap and excessive debt.

To begin with, let it be stated that, in the present financial system, money does not come into existence unless someone, individual, corporate or the state, agrees to go into debt, for that is the essence of the debt based financial system. And debts, invariably, have to be secured by collaterals.

"The global (debt) crisis, however, was indeed made in America, despite the sins of its imitators and fellow travelers. ------- (It was) a debt–fed party marked by a consumer binge on imported goods and the strutting of an ostentatious new class of super rich, who had invented nothing and built nothing except intricate chains of paper claims that duller people mistook for wealth". – TWO TRILLION DOLLARS MELTDOWN – C.R. MORRIS.

The Collateral creation exercise had its origins in the original mortgages over houses which are considered prime security given that it value increases over time with corresponding increase of owner's equity in the property as a consequence of repayments of due installments during the tenancy of the related facility. And given that majority of the people in these advanced economies have NEGATIVE PERSONAL NETWORTHS, their infinite gluttony for consumer goods and services encouraged them to pawn whatever unencumbered assets they had to raise additional financing by way of debt. Here the SHYLOCK, operating the Shadow Banking System (principally the investment banks) was waiting for his victim, who had money resources available in abundance in the form of highly leveraged hedge funds (100 to 1), sovereign wealth funds, pension funds, foundations and endowments. Some lenders offered financing to monetize owner's equity in the property by way of 2nd mortgage, others offered to have a fresh mortgage created on the property at higher market values, allowing the existing outstanding mortgage to be liquidated from funds released under this new mortgage; yet some bought up these outstanding mortgage loans from mortgage – banker intermediaries, whose loan book, as a result, were fully / partially cleared of mortgage related debts – in the process providing them with liquidity to contract further loans. This shadow banking system managed to by-pass the regulator, whose supervision was already at the minimum under the deregulated formal banking system, by recourse to off-balance sheet conduits.

Wall Street, having acquired the services of Ph.D.'s in Mathematics, came up with complex, structured financial instruments which were beyond the comprehension of bank's managements, who were content to go along so long as they got huge profit bonuses these schemes earned by way of commissions. The credit rating agencies too were befooled, given lack of independent investigations, in rating these products as investment grade. And the regulators, ofcourse in their free market mindset, did not question the merits and consequential risks of these so called investment grade products.

The sub-prime mortgage bubble commenced its fateful journey when shadow banking enterprises stepped in by buying original residential mortgages from prime lenders liquefying the local lending markets. They in turn, to maintain their liquidity, engaged in creating and selling mortgage based securities through Trusts created for the purpose. These trusts, in turn, issued 'certificates (bonds) representing a prorate slice of all the principal and interest it receives' – a process called securitization.

These were then marketed as Collateralized Mortgage Obligations – CMO-where the mortgages were sliced or trenched horizontally into segments with different bond for each segment splitting the risk and return for each segment of bond accordingly. The complexity of CMOs, which took a mainframe computer a whole weekend to model, spirited into an absurdity. Ultimately these mathematicians, with their doctorates and computers, went to the edge of lunacy in their mathematical constructs in introducing even more complex derivatives (options and futures) and finally with portfolio insurance as the ultimate backup in case of default. The latter appeared in the name of Credit Default Swaps, the riskiest of all. *Morris States, "a new class of arcane credit derivatives, completely outside the purview of regulators, ensure that almost all bank portfolios are 'tightly coupled' as engineers say, so failure in any part of the system will quickly propagate through the rest. An evil genie could not have designed a structure more prone to disaster."*

These, so called fictitious collaterals, were ultimately offloaded to the Hedge funds, off-balance sheet entities called SIVs and the like. Hedge funds, for instance, were excessively leveraged and when 'margin calls' on these could not be met, the rating agencies downgraded the related instruments leading to a market scare which prompted recall of credit lines leading interbank lending to a grinding halt. Consequently, this led to a domino effect throughout the financial system. Citibank, a bank which claims it never sleeps, had billions of long term loans in mysterious off-balance sheet entities which compelled its CEO, GARY CRITTENDEN, to make an admission to the effect that he. did not know how to value these new complex instruments. Lack of liquidity forced Federal Reserve to pump in new money to avoid the collapse. Unconventional methods were employed in the exercise, when these fictitious collaterals (Toxic Assets) were exchanged for Treasury Bills and the borrowing window was opened to entities which were not banking companies and had no right of recourse to Fed as lender of last resort. The liquidity crisis could not be contained despite all out efforts of the Fed, forcing the Federal Government to intervene to stem the rot, by injecting tax payers money to shore up banks depleted capital base, as co-equity holder. So much for the 'Deregulated Market Economy' hype that was the new found idol of the West. In this we see the 'self destruct mechanism' of Deceptive Money and Deceptive Collateral Creation in its full glory and play.

Western governments too were borrowing huge amounts from the banking system against their IOUs – Treasury Bills, with America, of course, the flag bearer, running a combined twin deficit (Trade & Budget) of over US$ 1.5 trillion annually, to support lavish living style, welfare economy and unending wars in the East. All this has combined to cause recession across the western hemisphere, leading to progressive dismantling of their welfare economic structures, where severe austerity measures, to contain their budget deficits, have been put in place, like in Greece, Portugal, Ireland, Iceland and Britain. USA is at the brink of its national debt limit, imposed by Congress, facing the spectre of government closure should the legislative body continue in its present stand.

To SUMMARIZE, the **Inverted Pyramid of Money Creation** with real savings representing the small inverted apex, supported by an equally **Inverted Pyramid of Fake Collateral Creation,** with a small base at the apex, of real securities in the form of residential mortgages over houses, have jointly created huge credit bubbles, essentially speculative in nature, which are not sustainable as recent history evidences causing severe economic dislocation both for the individual and the state, with Money Lords presiding over the financial apocalypse unmoved. It is something fundamental in the essence of

Money Lords to stand aside from creation proper and devote themselves to the money side exclusively.

As the brightest minds worked to produce this financial holocaust, *Nietzsche* had well noted that, *"Education is the art of deception; it produces clever devils"*. A fundamentally unsound monetary system, as we now have, will have to give way to a more reformed and regulated system, where money would seek its source in genuine savings rather than debt. To do so, the economy would have to be productive rather than speculative.

"The connection with barter, where commodities of equal value change hands, was preserved in the precious metal money. The principle underlying it was perfectly correct to the principles of modern physical science. Since wealth cannot be created out of nothing, but as a product of human effort expended on the raw material and sources of energy of the globe, no individual should be able to manufacture a new money claim to wealth out of nothing, and the purchaser should give up something equal in value to that which he so acquires. It is in this vital point that the modern method of multiplying claims to wealth fail".

Professor – F. Soddy.

In the growth of 'exchange mechanism' from barter to money, the latter was intended 'as an authorized token of the indebtedness of the whole community to the individual possessing the token' where the state represented the community – hence the legal tender money issued by the state. And the question is, why should this token be borrowed into existence?

In conclusion, I quote hereunder the most powerful and forthright warning ever made concerning the power of banking by *LORD JOSIAH STAMP, FORMER DIRECTOR OF THE BANK OF ENGLAND.*

"The modern banking system manufactures money out of nothing. The process is perhaps the most astounding piece of sleight of hand that was ever invented. Banking was conceived in iniquity and born in sin. Bankers own the earth; take it away from them, but leave them with the power to create credit, and with a stroke of pen they will create enough money to buy it back again -------. It you want to be slaves of the bankers, and pay the cost of your own slavery, then let the banks create money".

Chapter VIII

Implementation

"Those who understand economics do not recognize how well they understand economics, while professional economists imprisoned by text book knowledge have little understanding of economics and probably end up doing more damage than good."

GREENSPAN – *Former Chairman Federal Reserve Bank –*
New York

To implement the recommendations of this book, the following is suggested:

Phase 1: <u>Announcement to Parliament for amending section 24 of the State Bank of Pakistan Act 1956.</u>

With a view to curtail the national debt, in local currency, incurred by the Federal Government and the resultant debt servicing costs, the Federal Government is pleased to announce that Legal Tender money shall henceforth be issued by the Government of Pakistan in exercise of its sovereign right to issue currency as a neutral medium of exchange. Accordingly section 24 of the State Bank of Pakistan Act 1956 reading:

"----- **provided that the currency notes of the Government of Pakistan supplied to the bank (SBP) by the government may be issued by it for a period which shall be fixed by the Federal Government on the recommendation of the Central Board"**
is hereby amended to read instead:

"------ **provided that the currency notes of the Government of Pakistan will be issued by it (GOP) and supplied to the State Bank of Pakistan for circulation to the public through the banking system, in replacement of currency notes issued by State Bank of Pakistan. These notes issued by the Government of Pakistan shall exclusively act as the legal Tender money of the Islamic Republic of Pakistan".**
The change over / replacement exercise is to be completed within 12 months from the date of the approval of the amendment by parliament by simple majority.

Phase II : <u>Monetary Policy basic declaration to be announced by the State Bank of Pakistan.</u>

The basic guideline for the implementation of the monetary policy would hence-forth be the maintenance of equality between the

GROSS DOMESTIC PRODUCT (GDP), at current prices, to the aggregate STOCK OF MONEY, as determined with reference to M2;

$$\text{i.e., GDP, at current prices,} = M_2$$

The aforesaid finds its rationale in the latest historical research by professor Milton Friedman which showed that VELOCITY OF CIRCULATION, in the standard Quantity Theory of Money where money supply is the product of stock of money times its turnover rate, was found to be roughly constant, implying that what matters in the money supply equation is the aggregate money stock which if expanded at appropriately the rate of economic growth would leave prices roughly constant.

The Report of the Committee on the Working of the Monetary System of UK-'The Radcliffe Report' had made the following observations on the issue of VELOCITY OF CIRCULATION.

"We have not made more use of the concept because we cannot find any reason for supposing, or any experience in the monetary history indicating that there is any limit to the VELOCITY OF CIRCULATION. It is a statistical concept that tells us nothing directly of the motivation that influences the level of total demand."

Phase III : <u>Redemption</u> / Liquidation of government's domestic Floating and Permanent Debt.

The Ministry of Finance, in association with State Bank of Pakistan, will gradually implement a methodology to progressively redeem and /

or prematurely liquidate, as deemed appropriate, all government financial debt instruments, in the form of Treasury bills, Federal Government Investment Bonds and any other government debt obligation, of all types, classifications and tenors, by issuance of Government of Pakistan notes SAVE prize bonds and the unfunded debt with National Savings & Post Offices.

Concurrently with the aforesaid exercise, State Bank of Pakistan will implement a proportionate reduction in Statutory Liquidity Reserve Requirements (SLR) for the banks, ultimately abolishing it altogether and correspondingly increasing the Cash Liquidity Requirements (CLR) for the banks against current accounts, ultimately leading to 100% cash liquidity requirement against current accounts, with the aim of ensuring, at all times, the parity between GDP, at current prices, and money stock M_2.

Phase IV : <u>Redemption</u> of Prize Bond Scheme.

Given that the prize bond scheme has been the principal vehicle of whiting the black (undeclared / untaxed) money and supporting the underground economy, this scheme be redeemed by the issuance of Government of Pakistan notes.

With the completion of all the four phases detailed above, Government of Pakistan domestic national debt (permanent and floating) will stand liquidated with very substantial savings on account debt servicing costs SAVE the unfunded debt at National Savings and the Post Offices. All additions in legal tender money, which will, henceforth, not be borrowed into existence, save debts under National Savings and Post Offices, but will now come into existence, by the issuance of Government of Pakistan notes, in due proportion to the growth of the economy, represented by the increase in GDP. The inflationary factor arising from ever increasing government borrowings in the domestic money market will substantially be controlled, simultaneously affording the financial space to the private sector for raising credit from the banking sector, now that the state will be a non-entity in this market and will not stand accused of crowding out the private sector – the real engine of economic growth.

The gross public domestic debt (National debt) as of 30th June, 2010 was standing at Rs.4.6 trillion of which floating debt was at Rs.2.4 trillion (51.5% of gross debt) and permanent debt at Rs.794 billion (17% of gross debt) – cumulative debt, floating permanent, representing 68.6% of total gross debt. The maximum period for liquidating floating debt will be 12 months from the proposed date of the implementation of the policy whilst the permanent debt, being of a longer maturity, will take a few years longer to be fully liquidated, if liquidation is intended upon maturity of this debt, by redemption, instead of its premature liquidation. The profile of domestic public debt for the period 1990 – 2010 shows that, of the aggregate domestic national debt, floating debt has progressively increased over the period from 27% to 51.5%; permanent debt progressively reduced from 38% to 16% whilst unfunded debt ranged between 25.5% to 49%. The savings on account of debt servicing cost @ 14% pa arising from liquidation of floating and permanent debt – aggregate Rs.3.2 trillion would be in the region of Rs.448 billion annually. It is to be noted that gross public domestic debt (National debt) has, in absolute terms, continued its steep increase, year by year, starting at Rs.379 billion (1990) and rising to Rs.4.7 trillion (2010), never once recording a comparative fall from any of the previous years. This implies that national debt is, in essence, never reduced but continues to grow year by year. To replace it by government of Pakistan notes, the benefits that will accrue to the national economy will be (1) substantial savings on account of debt servicing cost (ii) the massive reduction in the absolute figure of national debt outstanding.

Where the component of 'currency' in the broader money supply M2 will show an increase, resultantly, there will be countervailing reduction in the second component – Deposit Money, of M2, because of reduction in SLR and increase of CLR. The latter exercise will, of course, call for SBP's expertise in managing the Money supply in compliance of new proposed Monetary Policy paradigm.

Reduction in 'National debt' coupled with improved tax collection, will provide the necessary financial space for the growth of economy, unimpeded by interference of IMF in matters domestic which should be the exclusive preserve of local money managers. Budget deficits, where occasioned, need to be financed from savings, attracted through National Savings Schemes and by issuance of Government of Pakistan notes ensuring the overall parity between GDP, at current prices and broader Money supply indicator M2.

A policy of near full employment should be pursued – educated youths be inducted in NADRA, NATIONAL SAVINGS, and UTILITY STORES, which institutions need to be strengthened and have their scope widened to provide efficient services both to the public and the state. Nadra's CNIC should have its data base further enhanced so that it should form the basic, all encompassing, individual identification; National Savings should form the principal avenue for the government for attracting savings from individuals to support / fund national development and utility stores to meet basic requirements of food and clothing at reasonable cost to the public and where extreme food shortages are encountered, to act as the 'ration' implementing agency on the basis of CNIC which be operated as 'ration card' at these outlets.

With external debt / liabilities standing at $ 56 billion (2010), IMF aggregate debt outstanding is (approx) US$ 8.07 billion (a mere 14.52 %) of the total external debt / liabilities. And with this contribution to external debt, it has taken over the whole national economy, dictating budgetary allocations, interest and exchange rate policy and a whole range of policy prescriptions in the economic field to the detriment of the national populace. IMF assistance, if essential, should be restricted to funding, on temporary basis, the balance of payment deficits with intervention, if at all, restricted to policy issues limited to international trade and no more.

World Bank and Asian Development Bank's project related financing must have these agencies assume 'credit and exchange risks', in due proportion with the Government and project concerned. Repayment installments must be adjusted to the principal in the first instance and interest, computed on outstanding principal balances, to be repaid at the end of the Amortization period, with provisions for waivers in case of need or where circumstances so warrant.

The concept of ODIOUS DEBTS needs to be studied and researched for incorporation as national policy with respect to external loans outstanding and where necessary and justified by facts, be litigated against in the International Court of Justice based on the principle established by USA with respect to 'Takeover' of Cuba from Spain and the refusal of USA to discharge Cuba's debts outstanding to Spain on the grounds of 'odious debt'.

Chapter IX

Review of Related Statistics

"There are lies; then there are white lies and to top it all, there are statistics."

Statistics related to :

(i)   State Bank of Pakistan's Issue Department – Notes issued and Assets backup;

(ii)   Domestic Public Debt;

(iii)   External Debt;

(iv)   Monetary Statistics – Money Supply & Currency (notes);

(v)   Relationship between gross domestic product (GDP), Broader Money Supply (M2) and Aggregate Domestic Debt;

Money Banker's Deception

for the period 1972 – 2010 (except for external debt which is covered for the period 1998 -2010) and a brief commentary on each follows in pages hereafter.

These statistics are extracted from State Bank of Pakistan publication Hand Book of Statistics on Pakistan Economy.

SBP's Issue Department - Notes Issued & Assets backup (Million Rupees).

Years	Notes issued O/s	Gold	FEX	Securities	Gold *	FEX*	Securities*
1972	8,105	649	1,429	4,236	8%	18%	52%
1973	10,412	649	2,403	5,754	6%	23%	55%
1974	10,546	649	2,417	5,962	6%	23%	57%
1975	11,642	649	2,957	6,686	6%	25%	57%
1976	13,308	662	4,409	6,571	5%	33%	49%
1977	16,757	662	2,456	12,835	4%	15%	77%
1978	19,605	3,053	5,798	9,470	16%	30%	48%
1979	25,248	4,765	1,927	17,102	19%	8%	68%
1980	29,178	11,547	4,239	12,290	40%	15%	42%
1981	36,362	7,644	7,186	20,616	21%	20%	57%
1982	39,279	7,025	6,725	24,555	18%	17%	63%
1983	47,368	10,016	21,366	15,037	21%	45%	32%
1984	53,724	9,550	18,663	24,455	18%	35%	46%
1985	58,858	9,490	6,051	42,385	16%	10%	72%
1986	65,636	11,080	12,629	40,741	17%	19%	62%
1987	77,792	14,791	12,389	49,241	19%	16%	63%
1988	91,205	15,022	7,079	67,777	16%	8%	74%
1989	100,918	15,077	7,001	78,426	15%	7%	78%
1990	118,515	14,702	10,411	92,099	12%	9%	78%
1991	142,170	17,148	8,275	115,285	12%	6%	81%
1992	158,655	17,153	11,949	113,093	11%	8%	71%
1993	175,719	20,499	3,619	135,319	12%	2%	77%

1994	196,029	23,897	54,147	101,461	12%	28%	52%
1995	229,313	24,260	70,008	118,547	11%	31%	52%
1996	250,620	27,116	32,381	174,664	11%	13%	70%
1997	259,363	27,519	21,332	193,850	11%	8%	75%
1998	289,997	27,833	18,716	225,757	10%	6%	78%
1999	305,326	27,614	75,279	184,270	9%	25%	60%
2000	373,738	31,002	60,153	264,472	8%	16%	71%
2001	393,114	35,617	111,027	243,187	9%	28%	62%
2002	458,374	39,378	245,300	170,389	9%	54%	37%
2003	522,891	41,246	459,116	18,558	8%	88%	4%
2004	611,903	47,532	514,138	45,671	8%	84%	7%
2005	705,865	53,870	472,513	162,802	8%	67%	23%
2006	784,236	76,317	561,728	135,585	10%	72%	17%
2007	893,293	99,127	699,199	108,830	11%	78%	12%
2008	1,050,148	133,004	147,248	456,071	13%	14%	43%
2009	1,231,652	203,345	463,693	718,353	17%	38%	58%
2010	1,386,195	212,737	478,236	712,412	15%	34%	51%

*Each as percentage of notes issued and outstanding.

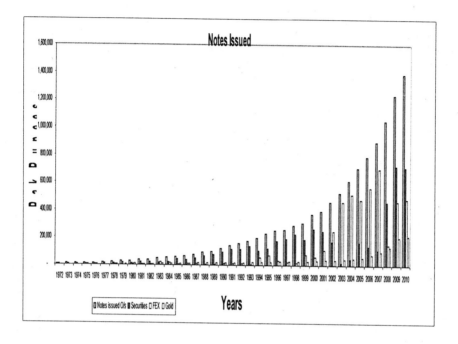

The above table shows the liabilities and major assets that make up the balance sheet of SBP's issue department. It is quite mysterious, on the part of SBP, not to publish the Profit and Loss Account of the issue department, whilst doing so for the banking department.

Notwithstanding, the above table reveals the aggregate growth of currency issued and outstanding for the period 1972-2010.

Of the assets backing the currency (liabilities) the largest component is the Securities (Treasury Bills); at times superseded by Foreign Exchange Reserves, whilst Gold remains the smallest component of the three moving within a narrow band. Securities and Foreign Exchange Reserves are both debt based whilst Gold is the only 'free asset' amongst the three components largely making up the asset side of the balance sheet. Foreign Exchange Reserves and Gold are both valued at current market prices -mark to market, and are both appreciating assets on account of rupee devaluation and increasing world gold prices respectively. The minimum and maximum of the three components with reference to currency issued and outstanding during the review period along with their averages are:

1) Gold, on average, was around 13% with highest at 40% & lowest at 3%

2) FEX, on average, was around 27% with highest at 88% & lowest at 2%

3) Securities, on average, were around 55% with highest at 78% & lowest at 4%

And the aggregate value of currency issued during the review period was Rs.8105 million (1972) and Rs.1,386,195 million (2010).

If the 'currency' were to be issued by the government of Pakistan not as debt but in exercise of its sovereign right to do so, as proposed earlier in the book, the 'securities' component will stand redeemed, Foreign Exchange Reserves, to the extent funded by direct government borrowings from IMF and other overseas sources to support balance of payment deficits, in cash, can be sterilized; whilst gold be kept as an unencumbered asset of the state.

DOMESTIC PUBLIC DEBT

Years	Total Debt	Permanent	Floating	Unfunded Debts
	A	B	C	D
1972	17,124	9,028	4,933	3,163
1973	19,811	9,222	6,949	3,640
1974	18,618	9,440	5,749	3,429
1975	22,520	10,334	8,123	4,063
1976	28,701	10,640	12,053	6,008
1977	35,344	10,783	17,737	6,824
1978	41,741	11,185	22,164	8,392
1979	53,469	12,666	31,160	9,643
1980	60,838	14,692	35,078	11,068
1981	59,124	15,172	31,688	12,264
1982	82,882	26,682	40,487	15,713
1983	105,362	33,369	48,554	23,439
1984	126,870	38,549	56,453	31,868
1985	155,407	39,357	73,087	42,963
1986	203,205	58,366	87,266	57,573
1987	249,189	69,057	104,885	75,247
1988	289,457	62,481	127,525	99,451
1989	332,523	76,953	135,238	120,332
1990	378,890	95,003	144,979	138,908
1991	445,041	151,757	150,928	142,356
1992	524,565	179,325	197,251	147,989
1993	605,184	234,657	215,819	154,708
1994	697,467	251,448	257,637	188,382
1995	794,204	275,681	294,233	224,290
1996	907,262	278,358	361,297	267,607
1997	1,048,076	281,279	433,833	332,964
1998	1,190,185	277,150	473,849	439,186
1999	1,375,906	256,928	561,590	557,388
2000	1,578,807	259,598	647,428	671,781
2001	1,730,989	281,077	737,775	712,137
2002	1,717,933	367,989	557,807	792,137
2003	1,853,675	427,908	516,268	909,499
2004	1,979,457	536,800	543,443	899,214

2005	2,152,286	500,874	778,163	873,249
2006	2,322,151	499,700	940,745	881,706
2007	2,600,635	552,972	1,107,656	940,007
2008	3,266,141	608,379	1,637,385	1,020,377
2009	3,852,566	678,048	1,904,009	1,270,509
2010	4,649,592	794,291	2,399,117	1,456,184

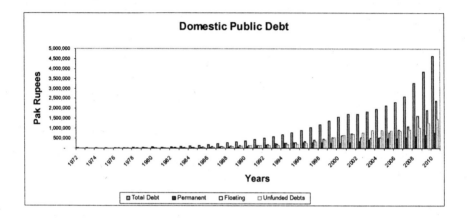

The aggregate domestic public debt ,which stood at Rs.17,124 million as of 30th June 1972 had escalated to Rs 4,649,592 million as of 30th June 2010. Whilst the floating debt has progressively increased it's share in the total debt from 29% (1972) to 52% (2010), Permanent Debt has correspondingly reduced it's share of total debt from 53% (1972) to 17% (2010). Unfunded debt, representing genuine public savings placed with the governmental agency -National Savings, has been fluctuating from a minimum of 18.5% (1972) of the total debt to a high of 31% (2010). Floating and permanent debt combined had been moving in the range of 69% to 82% of total debt. If the latter is redeemed by the issuance of Government of Pakistan notes -sole legal tender, as proposed earlier, a substantial reduction of national debt will be witnessed with savings in domestic debt servicing cost(estimated @14%PA) in the region of Rs 450 billion annually. This is equivalent to about 50% of budget deficit for the year 2011 - 2012.

External Debt

Years	Total External Liabilities	Public and Publically guaranteed Debt	Private Non Guaranteed Debt	IMF	Foreign Exchange Liabilities
	A	B	C	D	E
1998	33,596	25876	3127	1415	3178
1999	38,922	28347	3435	1825	5315
2000	37,860	27804	2842	1550	5664
2001	37,159	28165	2450	1529	5015
2002	36,532	29235	2226	1939	3122
2003	35,474	29232	2028	2092	2122
2004	35,258	29875	1670	1762	1951
2005	35,834	31084	1342	1611	1797
2006	37,229	35349	952	1491	839
2007	40,323	39832	1040	1407	818
2008	46,161	43078	1605	1337	1296
2009	52,331	48835	2290	5148	1274
2010	55,626	52107	2231	8077	1122

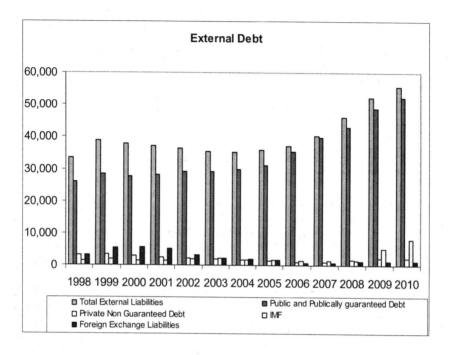

External Debt

External Debt which stood at about US 34 billion as of 30th June 1998 had shot up to about US 57 billion as of 30th June 2010 with IMF borrowings standing at US $8.07 billion. Liquidation, by progressive reduction, of this external liability, can come about only by having continuous surpluses on current account of balance of payments which appears to be an uphill task with the best of skills, competence and resolve, all of which seem to be, sadly, lacking. It is doubtful whether Pakistan would have the financial capacity of serving this debt from its own resources in foreign exchange without seeking more foreign currency loans to repay outstanding foreign currency liability. A severe belt tightening exercise is called for in our international trading activities to limit imports and increase exports, with a legally binding proviso that 20% of the gross proceeds from exports be set aside annually to redeem, progressively, the external debt liabilities (principal + interest).All privatization of state assets, where deemed necessary, in accordance with the unanimous decision of the Council of Common Interests of the federating units be offered for sale, only in foreign currency,[bids be invited in US dollar or other convertible currencies] and the proceeds so received should also be set aside to redeem external liabilities exclusively. The earlier an action on this front is taken the better, for otherwise the fate of GREECE in its current struggle to manage the sovereign debt crises, will befall Pakistan with even more severe consequences. When the MONEY LORDS can be so heartless to their own brethren in the West, can Pakistan avoid this Shylock when he demands his pound of flesh irrespective of the consequences. And do not forget that Shylock created his money out of thin air which he lent at interest and now demands real wealth, in the form of public assets and goods in return, at throwaway prices, of course!!

Monetary Statistic : Money Supply & Currency (Notes) (Rupees in Million)

Year	M2	Currency Issued	Currency in Circulation	Currency in Bank's Till	Currency Issued % of M2	Currency in Circulation % of Currency Issued	Currency in bank's till % currency issued
1972	22,059	8,105	5,173	498	37%	64%	6%
1973	27,068	10,412	7,286	577	38%	70%	6%
1974	30,679	10,546	9,295	729	34%	88%	7%
1975	33,074	11,642	10,273	833	35%	88%	7%
1976	41,651	13,308	12,603	1,012	32%	95%	8%
1977	51,773	16,757	15,523	1,679	32%	93%	10%
1978	63,659	19,605	18,310	1,654	31%	93%	8%
1979	78,612	25,248	23,745	2,060	32%	94%	8%
1980	92,424	29,178	27,649	2,187	32%	95%	7%
1981	104,621	36,362	34,750	2,515	35%	96%	7%
1982	116,510	39,279	37,650	2,665	34%	96%	7%
1983	146,025	47,368	45,767	3,020	32%	97%	6%
1984	163,267	53,724	52,039	3,004	33%	97%	6%
1985	183,905	58,858	56,447	4,087	32%	96%	7%
1986	211,111	65,636	63,276	4,101	31%	96%	6%
1987	240,024	77,792	74,703	4,623	32%	96%	6%
1988	269,514	91,205	87,785	5,135	34%	96%	6%
1989	290,457	100,918	97,508	4,984	35%	97%	5%
1990	341,251	118,517	115,067	5,351	35%	97%	5%
1991	400,644	142,170	136,967	7,339	35%	96%	5%
1992	505,569	158,655	151,819	8,962	31%	96%	6%
1993	595,390	175,719	166,864	11,301	30%	95%	6%
1994	703,399	196,029	184,708	13,738	28%	94%	7%
1995	824,733	229,313	215,579	16,363	28%	94%	7%
1996	938,680	250,620	234,110	19,328	27%	93%	8%
1997	1,053,234	259,363	244,141	17,821	25%	94%	7%
1998	1,206,320	289,997	272,922	18,769	24%	94%	6%
1999	1,280,546	305,326	287,716	18,870	24%	94%	6%
2000	1,400,632	373,738	355,677	19,468	27%	95%	5%
2001	1,526,044	393,114	375,465	19,178	26%	96%	5%
2002	1,761,370	458,374	433,816	26,414	26%	95%	6%
2003	2,078,705	522,891	494,577	30,415	25%	95%	6%

| 2004 | 2,486,556 | 611,903 | 578,116 | 36,432 | 25% | 94% | 6% |
| 2005 | 2,956,623 | 705,865 | 665,911 | 43,462 | 24% | 94% | 6% |

Money supply comprises of (i) Currency Notes (legal tender) and (ii) aggregate deposits with banking system or Deposit Money. Currency issued as a percentage of broader money supply M2 for the period 1972-2005 has progressively been reducing it's share of M2 from 34% to 25% , whilst aggregate deposits with banking system (a difference between M2 and currency) has been increasing correspondingly. Of the total currency issued, only about 6% is represented by 'cash in tills' with the banking system, the bulk (about 94%) remaining outside the banking system in possession with the public. It is obvious that 'cash' or 'currency' is not the principal source funding deposits. Then what is funding these deposits? The answer is obviously 'loans' through the mechanism of fractional reserve banking system. The above statistics are the living proof, if one is needed, how the banking system manufactures money out of thin air, where the 'loan' is the CAUSE and 'deposit' the EFFECT and not otherwise as it is conventionally misunderstood by the majority. It is this reality that has given rise to the 'debt based' economies worldwide where Money Lords rule supreme. Witness the Greek sovereign debt crisis and the role of European central bank, ECB, IMF and the credit rating agencies in forcing through severe austerity measures on the Greek population, practically dismantling the welfare economic structure of Greece.

Greece does not have the option of redeeming central bank issued currency-debt based by a non debt based government notes instead, as she does not have an independent control on currency issues, i.e EURO which is the currency of all participating EU member states minus UK, and is centrally controlled by ECB. What benefits does sovereignty grant to Greek parliament when 'money power' that resides outside its sovereign jurisdiction, dictates terms most inimical to Greece's citizens, merely to claim its pound of flesh?

Relationship between Gross Domestic Product (GDP), Broader Money Supply (M2), and Aggregate Domestic Debt.

Year	Gross Domestic Product (MP)	M2	Aggregate Domestic Debt	M2 % of GDP	Agg. Debt % of GDP	Agg. Debt % of M2
	A	B	C			
2010	14,668,428	5,777,231	4,649,592	39.39%	31.70%	80.48%
2009	12,739,336	5,476,873	3,852,566	42.99%	30.24%	70.34%
2008	10,242,799	4,791,898	3,266,141	46.78%	31.89%	68.16%
2007	8,673,010	4,406,846	2,600,635	50.81%	29.99%	59.01%
2006	7,623,205	3,679,033	2,322,151	48.26%	30.46%	63.12%
2005	6,499,782	3,201,870	2,152,286	49.26%	33.11%	67.22%
2004	5,640,580	2,731,049	1,979,457	48.42%	35.09%	72.48%
2003	4,875,648	2,266,163	1,853,675	46.48%	38.02%	81.80%
2002	4,452,654	1,927,995	1,717,933	43.30%	38.58%	89.10%
2001	4,209,873	1,650,125	1,730,989	39.20%	41.12%	104.90%
2000	3,826,111	1,476,675	1,578,807	38.59%	41.26%	106.92%
1999	2,938,379	1,316,989	1,375,906	44.82%	46.83%	104.47%
1998	2,677,656	1,262,522	1,190,185	47.15%	44.45%	94.27%

1997	2,428,312	1,170,525	1,048,076	48.20%	43.16%	89.54%
1996	2,120,173	976,156	907,262	46.04%	42.79%	92.94%
1995	1,865,922	865,798	794,204	46.40%	42.56%	91.73%
1994	1,573,097	771,871	697,467	49.07%	44.34%	90.36%
1993	1,341,629	649,249	605,184	48.39%	45.11%	93.21%
1992	1,211,385	583,894	524,565	48.20%	43.30%	89.84%
1991	1,020,600	435,882	445,041	42.71%	43.61%	102.10%
1990	855,943	341,251	378,890	39.87%	44.27%	111.03%
1989	769,745	290,457	332,523	37.73%	43.20%	114.48%
1988	675,389	269,514	289,457	39.91%	42.86%	107.40%
1987	572,479	240,024	249,189	41.93%	43.53%	103.82%
1986	514,532	211,111	203,205	41.03%	39.49%	96.26%
1985	472,157	183,905	155,407	38.95%	32.91%	84.50%
1984	419,802	163,267	126,870	38.89%	30.22%	77.71%
1983	364,387	146,025	105,362	40.07%	28.91%	72.15%
1982	324,159	116,510	82,882	35.94%	25.57%	71.14%
1981	278,196	104,621	59,124	37.61%	21.25%	56.51%
1980	234,179	92,424	60,838	39.47%	25.98%	65.82%
1979	194,915	78,612	53,469	40.33%	27.43%	68.02%
1978	176,334	63,659	41,741	36.10%	23.67%	65.57%
1977	149,748	51,773	35,344	34.57%	23.60%	68.27%
1976	130,364	41,651	28,701	31.95%	22.02%	68.91%
1975	111,183	33,074	22,520	29.75%	20.25%	68.09%
1974	88,102	30,679	18,618	34.82%	21.13%	60.69%
1973	67,492	27,068	19,811	40.11%	29.35%	73.19%
1972	54,673	22,059	17,124	40.35%	31.32%	77.63%

The above chart shows the gross growth of GDP, at market price, M2 and aggregate domestic debt and relationship amongst each other from the period 1972-2010. Whilst GDP(mp) has grown from rupees 54,673 million (1972) to rupees 14,668,428 million (2010), M2 has grown from rupees 22,059 million to rupees 5,777,231 million, implying that more goods and services are chasing less money-a deflationary situation. In percentage terms, M2 vis-a-vis GDP (mp) has ranged between about 40% to 50%. If we are to assume that aggregate money stock M2 is to maintain an equality with GDP (mp), i.e, the medium of exchange must be sufficient to the value of goods and services in an economy, to avoid inflationary/deflationary consequences, of excess money chasing few goods and vice versa, it is apparent that sufficient space is available for the expansion of total money stock, which can support higher level of economic activity by encouraging employment and the consequential higher growth without impacting inflation.

As for aggregate domestic debt vis-a-vis GDP (mp), this ranges generally between 40% to 30% showing a progressive decrease over time. Should the aggregate domestic debt decline, in absolute terms, given implementation of the proposal to switch public domestic debt represented by T bills and other government securities with government currency notes, a comfortable situation of total debt vis-a-vis GDP (mp) will be witnessed (total debt is equal to domestic debt combined with external debt).

It will, therefore, not be difficult to anticipate, with respect to Domestic Economy, an economic environment of high growth, near full employment, with low aggregate public domestic debt- latter financed principally from genuine public savings, provided the central authorities realize the critical nature of money- a neutral medium of exchange to come into existence under states' sovereign authority to issue currency-legal tender rather than to borrow it into existence.

Conclusions

- The currency notes (legal tender) issued by the State Bank of Pakistan, comes into existence as debt.

- The currency notes (legal tender) represents about 25% of the broader money supply aggregate M2.

- Over a period of time from 1972 to 2010, the currency notes (legal tender) as a percentage of M2 has progressively been declining in its aggregate share from about 34% to about 25% of broader money supply M2.

- The second component of money supply, namely deposit money, which comes into existence as banker's deception, money created out of thin air, is proportionally increasing its share in M2 over time from 66%to 75%.

- Of the aggregate currency notes (legal tender) issued and outstanding, a mere 6% - 7% of it is represented as cash in bank's tills; the remaining 94% - 93% being in circulation with public at large and outside the banking system.

- The currency notes (legal tender) are backed by assets comprising of :

1. Government securities (in fact IOUs issued by the government).
2. Foreign exchange reserves.
3. Gold.

Over a period of time, 1972 to 2010, government securities, in this regard, have fluctuated between 55% to 78% of the aggregate currency notes (legal tender) issued and outstanding whilst foreign exchange reserves between 27% to 88% and gold between 13% to 40%.

- The aggregate domestic public debt has increased in absolute terms, during the period from 1972 to 2010 (Rs 54,673 mn to Rs 14,668,428 mn) and represents 31.70% of GDP as of June 2010 and 80.48% of the broader money supply M2.

- Broader aggregate money supply M2 as of June 2010 stands at Rs. 5,777,231 Mn. Vis-à-vis GDP at Rs. 14,668,428mn, that is 39.39% of GDP at current market price.

- In consideration of price stability equation, that is the equality where M2=GDP(MP), as proposed by me, there appears substantial monetary space (Rs 8,891,197 mn &60.61%) for the expansion of money supply which will no doubt provide impetus for the growth of domestic economy all round. And if this expansion comes about, not as debt but as the state's sovereign right to create debt free money, there will be substantial advantage in reducing the debt service cost to the economy, in aggregate, as well.

Post Script- European Sovereign Debt Crisis

Although I had concluded writing this book by the middle of 2011, the re-appearance of global debt crisis in the form of European Sovereign Debt crisis has compelled me to add this postscript by way of a practical manifestation of the main theme of the book- that is, the crisis of debt based financial system, which seeks its rationale on banker's deception in the process of money creation.

The European Monetary Union-EMU- said to have been put in place by the BILDERBERGER GROUP, is indeed a strange animal. The union comprises of 17 member states, **"having a 'single currency'- the EURO that is not backed by political sovereignty. The 'zone' has a central bank called THE EUROPEAN CENTRAL BANK- ECB- that does not act as a lender of last resort nor does it finance government borrowings,"** a common function of central banks worldwide.

[Quote by Riccardo Bellofiore- Professor of Economics- Bergamo University, Italy.]

Each member country of the euro zone has the independence to formulate its fiscal policy and consequently the annual budget provisions as there is no significant centralized european public budget. In monetary policy, however, it has no such independence given a single currency, for the zone, and a centralized central bank-ECB.

The sovereign debt crisis of Greece had its origin in the budget deficits which were financed by borrowings from commercial banks against the security of uncollateralized government bonds. Given steep increase of Greece's public debt to GDP ratio, apprehensions began to be cast by the lenders as to the sustainability of Greece's public debt profile and hence the sovereign debt crisis. This crisis in reality is a private debt crisis resulting from privatized Keynesianism which allowed mixing of institutional funds, capital asset inflation and consumer debt- a model developed by USA and exported to Europe which led to an overall debt explosion.

Ordinarily, a country has recourse to printing of its money via the process of borrowing from its central bank when confronted with immediate bankruptcy/ default with commercial lending banks and increase in interest rates coupled with devaluation of its currency with a view to increase exports in the realm of monetary policy supported with fiscal measures of tax increases and curtailment of state expenses. However, given the unique split of control of monetary & fiscal policies between ECB and the state respectively, within the euro zone, the monetary policy option is simply not available with the participating member of the euro zone, in its individual capacity. Consequently, the financial assistance offered by ECB. IMF & EU to Greece, in surmounting its sovereign debt crisis, is primarily conditioned to severe austerity measures in the control of budget deficits which are having a telling effect on the general welfare of its citizens, correspondingly curtailing growth and giving an impetus to growing recession negating the financial targets set up with respect to corrective measures introduced as part of the conditionality for the financial assistance provided –the bailout packages, so to speak. In fact, what we are witnessing is a vicious cycle in operation where the conditionalities are accentuating the problem rather than improving the financial capacity of the state so that outstanding national debt obligations could be serviced and redeemed. Greece is bound to default sooner or later despite the financial cosmetics that are in the works because DEBT, per se, is not going to disappear in its essence but will merely be transferred first from private to public and now with ECB, IMF & the EU. If debt is liquidated in part or whole , it will contract money supply which will result in flat or negative growth, for it has to be understood that money has its origins in debt in the current economic system- NO DEBT NO MONEY ! A like situation is expected with respect to sovereign debt outstanding of Portugal, Ireland, Spain and Italy –participating members of the euro zone. The only remedy possible for saving the situation from total collapse is the writing off of debts by the lenders and starting afresh under a new economic paradigm. Lending bankers ought to take the hit, for the money they are now claiming was in fact created by them simply out of thin air, by the process of fractional reserve banking system, and does not represent public savings in any meaningful way. And in their greed, the lending bankers had thrown overboard all caution, indulging in reckless risk assessments, and allowed false prosperity for nations and individuals based on debts which were simply not serviceable. As they say that finally the chickens are coming home to roost, in response to banker's deception!

Across the Atlantic, facing Europe resides the Global King, United States of America, which, of late, has been displaying suicidal tendencies especially in its economic domain. Concerning its public debts, which makes UNCLE SAM the largest indebted nation on planet earth (it was a 'surplus' nation at the end of world war II) there was a lot of hue and cry at the approaching national debt limit, imposed by the Congress, which if not enhanced suitably, would have frozen all governmental activity in the United States and threatened its debt service capability on US government bonds held by domestic and international investors.

The brinkmanship displayed by Congress in withholding its approval till the very last critical stage ultimately led to down grading of American government's bond ratings, an instrument securing national debt, by a US based, leading ratings agency – an unthinkable outcome for world's leading reserve currency. This was the other side of the coin, called the sovereign debt crisis.

Whilst euro zone country has no recourse to monetary policy tools, in its individual capacity, the United States Constitution, article 1 section 8 part 5 provides thus:

Congress shall have the power to coin money and regulate the value thereof .

With this power vested with the Congress, as a constitutional obligation, one cannot comprehend the rationale of US government borrowing money, and thereby creating a national debt with obligation of its servicing and redemption, paid through by public taxes, to continue its functions.

Has the aforequoted article escaped the attention of the Congressman? Certainly not! For we have two leading examples during the administrations of President Lincoln and President Kennedy, where the aforesaid provision was resorted to.

The first is the famous case of GREENBACKS issued as treasury notes by the US government under the administration of President Lincoln not as debt but in exercise of its sovereign right to issue currency. Lincoln had resorted to this course, as an alternative, to finance Unionist's effort in the American civil war, where Money Lords were financing both sides of the conflict (Unionists & Confederates) @ 20%-25% interest per annum. Upon introducing his monetary policy, senate document 23 p 91-1865, based on the aforesaid, he met an assassin's bullet a few weeks later.

The second example is that of President Kennedy, when, on June 4, 1963, he signed an executive order 11110, a virtually unknown presidential decree, which had the authority to strip the Federal Reserve Bank of its power to loan money to the United States federal government at interest, essentially putting the privately owned Federal Reserve Bank out of business. The order returned to the federal government, specially the treasury department, the constitutional power to create and issue currency without going through the privately owned Federal Reserve Bank. President Johnson reversed the order on board airforce one while flying from Houston to Washington after the assassination. Some conspiracy theorist believes this executive order was the cause of President Kennedy's assassination.

Why did President Obama, a diehard follower of Lincoln, not resort to the example set by his above named predecessors when the republican majority Congress was being so inflexible with regard to the proposal to enhance the national debt limit? Perhaps, he does not suffer from the 'Taliban's Itch' for having an unscheduled early meeting with his Creator.

Just to give the reader a perspective of the debt levels in advanced economies it is said that the ratio of debt to GDP over the past 30 years has risen from 167 percent in 1980 to 314 percent today, where governments account for 49 percentage of the increase, corporations 42 percentage and household 56 percentage of the 30 year rise in debt levels. In USA, the household sector debt had, by 2007, jumped to 130 percent of personal disposal income and has recently come down to 115 percent. And then it is said, by all and sundry, that in banking savings fund deposits. If this were true, the world's advanced economies would not be in the dire straits that they are in presently.

To address the issue of unsustainability of debt worldwide, money needs to be created solely by the state, in exercise of its sovereign right to do, as legal tender exclusively, to equal national gross domestic product at current prices. Growth needs to be financed from genuine savings to come from net disposal incomes based on the premise that the saver abstains from consumption during the tenor of his saving/investment to avoid duplication of purchasing power.

About the Author

Shahid Hassan, a graduate in Economics and International Affairs and an associate of the Institute of Bankers, has been a professional banker since 1968, having served the banking industry for 42 years, retiring in the year 2010 as Executive Vice President with Samba Bank (Pakistan) Limited.

He commenced his banking career in 1968 with English, Scottish and Australian Bank (ESA), an international trading bank at its head office in the City of London and moved to Australia and Newzealand Banking Group (ANZ) London upon ESA'S merger with ANZ. He left ANZ to join the London city office of First National City Bank (now Citibank) and upon breakup of Pakistan in 1971 returned to Pakistan and joined Australasia Bank Ltd- later merged to form Allied Bank of Pakistan Ltd (ABL), in its international banking department at head office in Karachi. In 1975, he took up a position with National Development Finance Corporation (NDFC) to set up their foreign exchange department, to handle the first International Development Association (IDA an affiliate of IBRD) credit line of US 30 million. He served the institution for 25 years, in senior positions, in its various departments and was awarded a gold medal- Excellence Performance Award- for negotiating, executing and utilizing Pakistan's first ever and only YEN bond private placement arranged for NDFC in association with Daiwa Securities, Tokyo in a principal sum of yen 3 billion in the year 1987.

He was an Adjunct faculty member at the College of Business Management (CBM) where he taught MBA electives in International Finance, Foreign Trade and Banking for 10 years (2000-2010) and Treasury and Fund Management for a few semesters.

He has now retired and lives in Karachi with his wife and two children.

Bibliography

TOPIC : MONEY

SODDY, FREDERICK	The Role of Money	London- George Routledge and Sons Ltd	1934
SODDY, FREDERICK	Wealth, Virtual Wealth & Debt	London- George Allen and Unwin Ltd	1938
FISHER, IRVING	100 % Money	New York- An Adelphi Publication	1935
GALBRAITH, JOHN KENNETH	Money- Whence it Come, Where it Went	London- Pelican Books	1976
HELLYER, PAUL	Goodbye Canada	Canada- Chimo Media Inc	2001
ROWBOTHAM, MICHEAL	Grip Of Death	Oxford Carpenter	1969
AHMAD, SHAIKH MAHMUD	Man and Money	Karachi- oup	2002
ARMSTRONG, GEORGE	Rothschild Money Trust	?	1940
COUGHLIN, REV.CHARLES	Money- Questions & Answers	?	?

		Palmdale CA.	
SEARCH, DR.R.E.	Lincoln Money Martyred	OMNI PUB	1935
COOGAN,		Palmdale CA.	
GERTRUDE M	Money Creators	OMNI PUB	1935
LIETEAR,		London-	
BERNARD	The Future Of Money	Century	2001
		England-	
		Universal	
PIDCOCK, SWAN	The Crash of 2008	Empire UK	2009
		London-	
HARROD, RF	Money	Macmillan	1969
		London-	
		Bloomfield	
DOUGLAS, C.H.	The Monopoly of Credit	public	1979
		Palmdale CA.	
ADAMS,S.W.	The Federal Reserve System	OMNI	1958
MULLINS,	The Secrets of Federal	USA Emissary	
EUSTACE	Reserve	Pub	1993
SUTTON,	The Federal Reserve	USA Emissary	
ANTONY. C	Conspiracy	Pub	1995
	What Everybody Really		
HUTCHINSON,	Wants to Know About	Oxford	
FRANCES	Money	Carpenter	1998

TOPIC : BANKING LAW

PAKISTAN LAW			
HOUSE	Banking laws	Karachi	1997
HOLDEN, J.	The Law & Practice of		
MILNES	Banking vol. 1	London- Pitman	1982

Banker/customer

MATHER, L.C.	Banker & Customer Relationship	London-Waterlow	1971
HAPGOOD, MARK	Paget's Law of Banking	London-Butterworth	1989
PLD 2000 SC 760	The All Pakistan Legal Decisions	Karachi	1999

TOPIC: INTERNATIONAL FINANCE

AHMED, LIAQAT	Lord of Finance	London- William Heineman	2009
SKOUSEN, W. CLEON	The Naked Capitalist	Emissary Pub.	1970
GRIFFEN, DES	Fourth Reich of the Rich	Emissary Pub.	1976
KORTEN, DAVID. C	When Corportations Rule The World	San Francisco-Kumarian press	2001
EINZIG, PAUL	The Euro- Dollar System	London-Macmillan	1973
SOROS, GEORGE	The New Paradigm for Financial Markets	New York-Public Affairs	2008
MORRIS, CHARLES R	The Two Trillion Dollar Meltdown	New York-Public Affairs	2008
TURNER, GRAHAM	The Credit Crunch	London- Pluto Press	2008
GALBRAITH, JOHN KENNETH	The Great Crash 1929	New York-Houghton Mufflin	1997
DOUGLAS , C.H.	Social Credit	Canada-Instistue of Economics	1924

		Democracy	
		London	
DOUGLAS , C.H.	Economic Democracy	Bloomfield Pub.	1974
		Washington-	
GOLD, JOSEPH	Standby Arrangments of IMF	IMF	1970
REIMANN,	The Challenge of	New York- Mc	
GUENTER	International Finance	Graw Hill	1966
ROWBOTHAM,		Oxford-	
MICHEAL	Goodbye America	Carpenter	1969

TOPIC: MONETARY HISTORY

QUIGLEY,	The Anglo- American	New York-	
CORROLL	Establishment	Books in Focus	1981
QUIGLEY,		New York-	
CORROLL	Tradgey & Hope	Macmilliam	1966
MARSDEN,			
GEORGE	The Protocols of Zion	?	1934
		New York-	
MARRS, JIM	Rule by Secrecy	Harper Collins	2000
REHMAN.		Islamabad- Mr.	
SHAHID UR	Pakistan Sovereiginity Lost	Books	2006
RODISON.		London-	
MAXIME	Islam and Capitalism	Pelicain Books	1966

TOPIC:INFLATION

		New York-	
FISHER, IRVING	Inflation	Adephi pub.	1935
WADSWORTH,	The Banks & Monetary	London-	
J.E.	System in UK	Methueu	1973

TOPIC: ECONOMICS

| LIPSEY, | An Introduction to Positive | London William | |
| RICHARD G. | Economics | cloves | 1963 |

TOPIC: HISTORY

| SPENGLER, | | New York- | |
| OSWALD | The Decline of the West | Modern Libarary | 1932 |